of Congress Catalog Card Number 93-83798

882885-01-5 (paper)
882885-00-7 (cloth)

consultant in art direction, Inge Christensen, Parker, CO
lustration, Sheryl Regester, Georgetown, CO

n Schools and Businesses:
y Princeton/Masters Press are available at quantity
s. For information, write: Princeton/Masters Press Inc.,
Maplewood, Suite 333, Englewood, CO 80111 or call 800-
6.

5 4 3 2 1

An Easi
to Chan

The Complete Prin
Job Changing Syst

An Ea
Gerbe
Reserv
book n
in the

Library

ISBN
ISBN

Primar
Cover

Attenti
Books
discour
7951 E
772-44

9 8 7 6

By Bob Gerberg

About the Author

Bob Gerberg has a BA degree from Colgate University and an MBA degree from the University of Pittsburgh. After several years as an Air Force Officer, he had a successful career with major food companies, including positions as a Vice President of Marketing and Assistant to the Chairman of a Fortune 500 company. Active in the career and outplacement fields for more than a decade, he has authored more than 2 dozen books, publications and cassettes on the subjects of job and career change.

This book will be updated annually. Suggestions or experiences with the system are welcomed by the author and can be sent to him at Box 370065, Denver, Colorado 80237.

About Princeton Masters

Princeton/Masters is an outplacement consulting firm with independently owned offices and associates in major cities. The firm's specialty is helping market professionals, managers and executives into new jobs and careers. The system presented in this book covers the basic marketing formula which guides the firm's professional staff. Depending on the nature of each individual assignment, the system is then tailored by consultants to fit each person's particular career situation and objectives.

I have always felt that the ability to change jobs or careers is of vital significance to a person's confidence and self-esteem, and, of course, their own career success and happiness.

This system is about a dramatically easier, more professional and more effective way to change jobs—one that has helped many others at all income levels and which can have a dramatic and positive impact on your life as well.

This book could not have been produced without the very special contributions of several individuals. My son, *Bob Gerberg Jr.* directed much of the design and development of this product and *The Princeton/Masters "Easier Way to Change Jobs Course"* simultaneously.

In both cases the goal has been to create a unique structure and format, one which facilitates superior communication of this material. Every effort has been made to make this book easy to read and use. Extensive use of humor and case histories, illustrations and graphics have been included to maximize your comprehension, enjoyment and potential ease of use.

The editorial and creative contributions of several professionals could also not go without mention. This includes five individuals, each of whom has devoted a good part of their careers to helping market people into new jobs. They are each pros in the best sense of the word, and the wisdom, experiences and creativity they have shared is greatly appreciated. My personal thanks to *Mallory Dean* and *Michele Lutz* in Denver, Colorado, *Charles Dimon* in Irvine, California, *Tom Smith* in San Ramon, California, *Bob West* in Houston, Texas, as well as the entire professional staff of Princeton/Masters.

I wish to also extend my appreciation to the many clients of Princeton/Masters whose successful experiences have translated into the underlying system which is now shared in this publication.

Bob Gerberg
Denver, Colorado & New York, N.Y.

Contents

Introduction
and Overview

There is no substitute for having a job you really enjoy

Millions of men and women are settling for jobs or careers that they no longer enjoy, and that bring them far less than they really want out of life. Nevertheless, having the right job can make you a different person than you were yesterday. It can affect your feelings, your mood, your family, your energy and even your whole outlook on life. It also changes the way you see yourself and the way others see you.

Unfortunately, when it comes to jobs and careers, most people in the world play it safe. They tend to underestimate themselves and therefore remain in jobs and careers that offer little future or excitement.

Worse yet, many are in positions which are dull, routine and unchallenging. These people have stopped growing. Furthermore, they won't grow simply because they won't give themselves a chance.

Why? Well, it's easier to stay with what is familiar rather than risk the unknown. It is also hard to overcome inertia and take that first step. However, one of the great lessons about jobs and careers is that almost every person has a reservoir of talents and skills that are unknown or untapped. What's more, this unused potential has been proven to exist at virtually all ages.

Interestingly, 77% of all employed professionals say that during the last year they have thought about finding a new job. Yet, most didn't really have the confidence that they could make a good move and never entered the job market.

Why do people finally decide to try and make a move? Here are the results from a survey of more than 4,000 employed but active job seekers, people who were looking for administrative, managerial, professional or executive jobs in early 1993. All had attended college. They were free to check any of the items below.

	Men (%)	Women (%)
Enjoy my job but wish to try something else	22	22
Blocked / need higher income *	21	39
Bored / unchallenged	19	21
Not enough enjoyment	15	17
In wrong field / industry *	15	4
Not enough responsibility	14	12
In danger of losing job	9	9
Company / industry contracting	9	9
Feel burned out	8	9
Bad political environment	8	6
Not enough independence	7	7
High pressure *	7	1
Low ego satisfaction	5	4
Not on fast track	4	6
Position was changed	4	4
Not getting along with boss	3	3
Passed over / lost out	3	3
Not in mainstream of communications *	2	11

* Factors on which there was a significant difference.
  This survey was comprised of equal numbers of men and women and people who were seeking to relocate were not included.

Most people lack confidence about job hunting because they only know approaches from the 1970s and 80s. What's more, they have no feeling for where the jobs really are.

The U.S. job market and how people look for professional level jobs today

Most people start by writing their resume. It is generally a "tombstone resume" saying "Here lies John Doe, born this day, went to these schools, had these jobs." Then, once they get their resumes together, they just scatter them as they answer some ads or visit a few recruiters or personal contacts.

Some send out mass mailings using poor materials, the wrong lists and the wrong techniques. In short, their approach is haphazard, full of dead end leads, and they end up job hunting for a long, long time.

Last year we did another survey among several thousand professionals, managers and executives who had made a job change within the past six months. What we found was not surprising. The vast majority felt that job hunting had been a difficult and lonely process in which they found their way by trial and error.

However, less than one in ten had approached job hunting with the same planning, effort or commitment that they routinely put forth in their jobs. Among those who made a change, here's how their traditional methods enabled them to find their positions.

59 % — from existing personal contacts and direct referrals from them;

22 % — from networking efforts outside of the above (indirect referrals);

9 % — by contacting or being contacted by agencies or executive recruiters;

3 % — through answering advertisements;

3 % — from contacting employers directly; and

3 % — by all other means (placing ads, through trade associations, university placement centers, committee searches, computer match services, etc.)

Among the executives in our survey who had been forced out of work via corporate downsizing and who did not have the benefit of private outplacement help, here was the average number of months from the date of their notification until they started in a new job.

Scientific .... 16.7 months
General management .... 13.7 months
Legal / consulting .... 12.6 months
Human resources .... 11.9 months
Accounting / finance .... 11.1 months
Misc. staff positions .... 10.9 months
Operations .... 9.9 months
Office management.......................... 9.4 months
Marketing / sales / P.R. .... 8.8 months
Engineering & related .... 7.3 months
Information systems .... 7.1 months

This was during a slow economy; however, the main reason it took them so long related to their lack of a professional marketing approach and dependence on their own contacts. Many of them were also in situations that dictated a change in careers or a move into a new industry.

Even though many had thought about making a move for 12 to 18 months, it was still surprising how many were caught short when finally faced with termination.

A friend of mine, an executive who was released after a very successful career with a large firm, told me that his advice to others was they should plan on being fired at least once by surprise. However, the fact remained that he had plenty of warning signs!

As I'm sure you know, geologists, architects and mechanical engineers are not the only ones who have had to find new careers or industries lately. Rather forced career changes have included professionals and middle managers in most major U.S. companies. Even growth companies are learning that periodic sweeping purges are required to cure problems of bad decisions and excess.

So, from your point of view, now might be the time to think about what you would do if you had to leave your field. Here's some rather simple advice, but it has worked as a launching pad for people at all ages and income levels.

Get involved in a new career or industry while you are employed. Build your knowledge base by becoming a professional consultant, contract worker or temp on a part-time basis, or start a small business with your spare time, either with family, friends or on your own. If necessary, work for a few months as an apprentice and perhaps even without income or on a modest commission.

Before long, you'll have developed the knowledge, experience and a new confidence, and you will be all set when it comes to new options.

Another interesting point emerged from our survey of professionals who lost their jobs. Even though their unemployment was costing them an average of between $3,000 and $12,000+ per month, relatively few invested more than several hundred dollars toward finding their new jobs!

Now, clearly, job hunting does not need to take as long as the data on the previous page suggests. However, in a recent major article, *Business Week* magazine said executives who lost jobs should plan on 18 months of unemployment, and the U.S. Labor Department has been widely quoted as saying it takes a year or more.

If your goal is to make the best possible career move, rather than simply getting a job, and if you want to do it faster than others, it's also important to have some perspective on where the opportunities are in today's market. During the last decade there has been a profound change in America. The most, and often the best, opportunities are with small businesses rather than the most famous corporations.

Among large firms, because annual turnover is estimated to be 25%, many positions are always becoming available. Nevertheless, if we discount acquisitions and mergers, the total employment in the country's 2,000 largest employers has declined over the last ten years.

Obviously, there will be many fine opportunities that become available with the nation's leading organizations. However, for the most part they will only occur from retirements, terminations and turnover.

On the other hand, despite the bad news reported in the business press, the fact is that the U.S. has hundreds of expanding industries. You may be aware of some of them, but a more comprehensive list of faster growing areas is provided in the last chapter of this book.

These industries have spawned the development of tens of thousands of fast-growing small businesses as well. This has remained true throughout the recession of the early 90s, and even better growth is expected for the rest of the decade.

One of the major problems for job seekers is that they cannot easily identify these organizations. Because of the expense, these employers are also far less likely to list their jobs with recruiters or to spend money on advertising them.

To explore the opportunities with these organizations you need to first identify them through your local press, computer databases or other research, and then contact them with the approaches outlined in our system. Since most people want to find new employment without having to relocate, the data on the next page will help give you some idea of the number of employers out there.

The chart below lists the number of employers as ranked by the number of full-time employees they have. The breakdown is quite typical of what you would find in most of the country's major metropolitan areas of comparable size.

Since well over 90% of all people who look for jobs want to continue to reside in their current areas, this will give you some idea of the number of employers out there for you—aside from the more well-known and larger organizations.

Obviously, the employers in the under-five category will be of little interest as these are mostly small retail shops and independents. However, the employers who have between five and 100 employees would include companies in many of America's newest and fastest growing industries.

Number of organizations according to the number of full-time employees in a specific location *			
	Under 5 Employees	**5 - 99 Employees**	**100 + Employees**
San Fran./Oakland Pop. 3.8 million	110,700	50,300	2,200
Houston Pop. 3.4 million	82,900	48,800	2,100
Denver/Boulder Pop. 1.8 million	53,400	30,300	1,400

* Data supplied by Contacts Influential, Inc.

The philosophy behind this system

To advance your career and life-style, chances are that timely job changing will play a critical role in your future success.

However, as already mentioned, with America's current economic position in the world, the number of attractive jobs with major employers has not been expanding. This is especially significant if you relate jobs to the continuously increasing numbers of people in the job market.

Consider the following: besides the half million new college graduates who are entering the market each year, the percentage of women seeking employment continues to expand; and people who are living longer are wanting to work longer.

Major employers will continue to downsize and thin middle management ranks for years to come. In this environment of faded corporate loyalty and much greater competition for good jobs, how should you position your career? What are your possible moves if things don't go right, and just how would you go about making it happen?

Up until now, most people have allowed their lives to be determined by jobs that simply come their way at a point in time. Typically, people engage in "passive" job hunting by waiting for ads to appear, for recruiters to call, or for contacts to give them a call about a job opening they hear about.

As a result, millions of talented people settle for less and are under-employed, simply because of their dependence on traditional job hunting methods. However, the revolution in personal computers, word processing, databases and other sources for information are having a dramatic impact on your job hunting alternatives.

They make it possible for you to take control of your own destiny instead of playing the waiting game. That is what the our philosophy is primarily about.

This system will give you a more scientific approach to maximizing every job hunting action you take. That includes our philosophy on exactly how you should answer ads, make use of recruiters, use references, handle your interviews, how you should negotiate and much more.

However, our system clearly emphasizes new and well-organized approaches for going to your markets, with the goal of uncovering the right opportunities within a less competitive environment. We call it "pro-active" rather than passive job hunting.

This system requires that you first develop your priority list of your universe of possible employers in your locale. That's not too much of a task, but it should be done according to type of industry, growth prospects and company size.

After that you map out a one-page plan-of-action for getting interviews, and subsequently use selective direct mail, telemarketing and networking to get face-to-face with decision-makers in those organizations.

Our system will also introduce you to a completely new method for writing the types of resumes and letters that will produce your best response.

Importantly, the requirements of our system are modest. You only need a couple of days to master the easy-to-read pages that follow.

Let's look at how professionals and executives end up finding their new jobs using the Princeton / Masters system. Keep in mind that people pursue many methods simultaneously for getting interviews, and they use them in conjunction with superior materials. The main thing about their efforts is they depend far less on their own contacts, as 90% find jobs via other avenues.

Typically, people using our system will develop interviews from all of the sources below. The chart only reflects the source that yielded the final job offer they accepted. *(See page 11 for how people traditionally find their positions.)*

10% **From existing personal contacts & direct referrals from them**

29% **By using our methods for networking (indirect referrals)**

19% **By using our methods for approaching recruiters**

9% **By using the Princeton/Masters' way for answering ads**

4% **By placing ads, appts., committee searches, university placements, trade associations, etc.**

29% **By using Princeton/ Masters' methods for direct to employer contact via direct mail or telemarketing and using spot opportunities**

What are the requirements for success with this system?

Succeeding with this system is up to you. However, it has already been successfully used by men and women of all ages and income levels. To make this system work, you need to be open to new ideas and willing to put aside your old ideas on job hunting. You also need to make a commitment to put the information into action.

Once mastered, this process will build your self-esteem and give you added confidence throughout your career. Making timely moves, instead of staying in limited-growth situations, can be your key to long-term success.

With this system at your finger tips, the most critical element for your success will simply be your own attitude, your will to succeed and your commitments to making the time available for doing it the right way.

When most people look for a job, they work on it five to six hours a week. Then, if you add the fact that they go out with the wrong materials and do all the wrong things, what can they realistically expect?

In spite of the competition, don't be misguided by old cliches that tell you to allow one month for every $10,000 you seek. With this system, you'll be doing more and doing it right. Experience has shown that you can cut your job hunting time in half, sometimes much more, and get far better results at the same time.

Whatever your own credentials, the major reason you can do much better is simple. *The other 98% who compete with you will be job hunting as usual.*

This system is truly an easier way to change jobs because you will be able to uncover a far broader range of options, better handle your liabilities, and encounter far less stress than people who approach job hunting the traditional way.

Section One:
This System and You

The first section will make sure you understand the basic principles of professional job search. There is nothing technical or complicated. The goal is to put you in control of the job hunting process by allowing you to take a series of planned actions in a common sense sequence.

Chapter One provides a brief overview of common sense fundamentals and takes just a few minutes to review. Chapter Two is important for everyone but especially for those who would like to change careers or industries.

Chapter

Professional Job Search:
A New Way to Find
the Right Job or Career

New Way

Old Way

This system involves finding the right options, marketing yourself according to a step-by-step action plan, telling a unique story with superior materials, and knowing how to project the right image and build personal chemistry.

A brief review of professional job search ... and how to do it

This system is basically a formula for professional job search. It involves using a planned approach to everything you do as part of your job campaign.

There are five broad stages to running a professional search. They include advance thinking about your marketability, assets and your options; development of an action plan for getting the right interviews; preparation of all the creative materials you will need; research on organizations to contact and action which involves interviewing and negotiating to the best of your ability.

Uncovering your assets, your career and industry options, and knowing how to handle any liabilities

The first thing you need to do is to make sure you uncover all your marketable assets. Too many people write a resume before they have ever really analyzed themselves and the full range of what they might be able to offer an employer in certain situations. In line with this, you need to make sure you uncover every saleable asset or experience you have.

To help you do this, review the discussion in *Chapter 2* on *"How to Uncover Everything That's Marketable About You."*

At the same time, you will want to review your career and industry options. People often view themselves solely by what they've done in the past. This causes them to approach job hunting from a very narrow perspective, as they never consider many new and viable options. However, every day men and women of all ages make moves into new careers, frontier industries and growth situations.

Many people have found that crucial career changes have changed their lives and brought them success and in some cases fame. Chances are, you can discover entirely new careers and industries, as well as advanced opportunities within your career path.

Many things covered in this system will encourage you about your options. Hopefully, the ideas will help inspire your own fresh thinking in this area.

Knowing how to get the right interviews and developing your own action plan

In today's competitive job market, you will never get enough interviews if you use a hit-or-miss approach. This is why it is important to prepare a step-by-step game plan. While it's important that you take the right actions in answering ads and using recruiters, your main focus should be on uncovering private job openings. It's the least competitive arena and it's also where most openings are.

With this system you'll be able to develop an action plan that's tailored to both the goals you have and the time you can devote to job hunting. After covering Chapters 3 through 9, review Chapter 10 and use it to formulate your own plan.

Preparing all your creative materials

Everyone in life will sooner or later write a resume, and most people can expect to revise it again and again as they go through their careers. Chapter 11 of this system will introduce you to an entirely new and highly effective philosophy for developing resumes. The difference between "average" resumes and the ones you can prepare with this advice can be extraordinary.

When your new resumes hit the marketplace, they can easily have 700% to 1,000% more impact than a traditional resume you might have created.

In many cases letters work much better than resumes for getting first interviews. Using the brief discussion on *Letters,* you will be able to quickly draft memos and letters that will help speed the implementation of your campaign. With them at your fingertips, you'll be ready for any situation that presents itself.

Identifying the right organizations to contact

Most people know that if they cannot get access to the right leads, all of their efforts may be in vain. Throughout this system you will be introduced to a variety of useful sources and many ways for identifying the right employers to contact. However, you should be sure to review Chapter 6 on *"Finding Unadvertised Jobs,"* and our last chapter for *Sources of Information."*

You will also want to gain access to the many databases that can enable you to sort and select potential employers to contact and to retrieve names, addresses, phone numbers, titles and the like. Developments in this area are making it possible to dramatically speed the telemarketing and direct mail efforts of almost any job search.

Getting into action: interviewing and negotiating

For every interview you go on, there are likely to be many people under consideration. So, obviously it's important for you to come across better than others. The most critical thing you need to do is to build personal chemistry with all the new people you will be meeting. In this book you'll find a series of seven steps which, if you follow, will allow you to maximize your chemistry in every interviewing situation.

In Chapter 2 on *Marketability,* you'll also be introduced to our concept of a personal "communications plan" and the importance of answering questions with interesting stories using our SODAR technique. This has helped others to perform at peak levels — and it will do the same for you.

It's also easy to perform well in any interview if you plan ahead regarding knowing what you want to say or not say, being ready for the questions you might be asked, and being ready with your own questions.

All of these things combined are part of what I call your "communications plan." Chapter 12 on *Turning Interviews into Offers* is all you need here.

Negotiating is very important, and you should never be afraid or intimidated by the process. Unfortunately, when most people receive an offer, they simply take it. The fact is that every year people leave millions of dollars on the bargaining tables of employers. However, keep in mind that if you are 35 years old and leave $10,000 on the bargaining table, your real loss may be $10,000 x 30, or $300,000 by the time you retire.

Chapter 13 of this book will introduce you to a comfortable and easy-to-use process for negotiating your best possible financial package. It has been all that many others have needed. I hope it will do the same thing for you.

The importance of having a positive attitude and making your very best effort

The knowledge this system will give you, along with a strong effort, will more than compensate for somewhat lesser credentials. However, a positive attitude is the single most common thread among all winners. It will separate you from the hundreds of thousands who simply give up, settle for less and remain in unattractive situations.

With this system at your fingertips, job hunting success is inevitable— it's only a question of when you make it happen. You may wish to review the discussion in Chapter 16 on *How to Build a Will to Succeed That Makes a Difference.*

How to Uncover Everything That's Marketable About You!

With this system your starting point is to never limit your view of yourself!

Your experience is more marketable than you might think

If you are like most people who want to make a major move, you probably think that your chances are a "long shot." However, once you face up to things and determine to do something about them, you have taken the first step toward resolving your career situation.

It has been said time and again by psychologists, motivational speakers, spiritual leaders and coaches, that the most restrictive limits you face are those you put on yourself. So, if you really want to be a serious candidate for a better position or a new career, don't put any limits on your thinking and be willing to go for it!

When it comes to job hunting, what everyone thinks of first is experience. However, most of us think of our experience in more narrow terms than we should. That type of thinking restricts our opportunities as many good situations pass by unnoticed.

As you go through this chapter, we will review a number of ways that will enable you to take a new view of your total experience and how you can describe it to potential employers.

Your knowledge is marketable

Make a list of things you know. For example, do you have knowledge of a job, a product, a process or a market? It could come from work, hobbies, schooling, reading, activities or from suppliers, customers, friends or your social life.

EXAMPLE #1— Consider the case of a 30-year-old office manager who decided she'd like to sell computer printers. She had no sales experience, but her knowledge of why some printers operated better than others convinced an employer to hire her as a sales representative.

EXAMPLE #2— In another instance, a food industry executive was offered the opportunity to head up a real estate development. What was the connection? Well, the real estate firm appreciated this executive's knowledge and ability to organize, which they perceived as their primary need.

Their decision to extend an offer, however, was based just as much on the fact that this executive had long shown an interest in real estate. Though by no means an expert in the field, she was familiar with trends in the industry, and they felt her interest would enable her to learn the business quickly.

EXAMPLE #3— A recent graduate with no work history other than summer jobs as a waitress was offered a job as Assistant to the Manager for a travel company. The reason for the offer? First, no one else had contacted this firm. Second, the industry knowledge she demonstrated during her interview helped. Where did she get that knowledge? By researching back issues of trade magazines.

Your personality and character may also be marketable

Personality, of course, is just a word for that mysterious combination of traits that can either attract us to someone quite strongly, or on the other hand, leave us unimpressed.

Many employment decisions have been based on personality. It happens thousands of times every day. When it does, the employer is probably thinking something like this:

"He's certainly a positive, quick-thinking fellow. I like him, and better yet, I trust him. He'll be able to get along with our people and provide leadership. I want him in this company, and I'm going to make an offer right now."

If most people seem to like you when they meet you, chances are you will meet people who have the power to offer you a position in a totally unrelated field.

"PERSONALITY" EXAMPLE— You don't have to settle for just a chance meeting, either. One homemaker was hired as an Administrative Assistant after four letters and three meetings with managers in a local company. Why was she hired? Well, it's true that no one else kept knocking on their door like she did, but what won them over was that everyone she met took a liking to her.

Don't ever forget that your character is also marketable. In fact, when it comes to choosing between other people, most decisions are made based on personal qualities. Having qualities of integrity, thoughtfulness and loyalty really count.

Depending upon your personal situation, characteristics like these may suggest a certain company, occupation or industry for which you would be particularly well suited. If some aspect of your personality makes you suited for certain types of activities, now is the time to investigate whether it might lead to a preferred career direction.

Your interests and enthusiasm are marketable

How many employers do you suppose have hired people principally because they showed a great deal of interest in their business? The answer is a lot!

"ENTHUSIASM" EXAMPLE — A packaging salesman was interested in medical equipment and was fascinated by advances to reduce back pain.

How did he win a position as VP for a three-year-old growth company in that field? Well, he answered an ad, just as 300 other applicants did. But he didn't stop there.

Over the next two weeks, he wrote four more letters to the president of that company. To each letter he attached his own thoughts of why the firm's equipment should win the major share of a particular market. To the last letter he attached his suggestions for new markets the company should consider.

His insights were not based on experience, but on his interest and casual reading of the industry's trade press over the years, combined with intensive study during the two weeks in which he wrote the letters. When the president made the offer, he volunteered that he'd seen plenty of candidates with more impressive credentials, but not one with a tenth as much enthusiasm.

The opportunity you represent is marketable

If you can make an employer aware of an opportunity that you can help exploit, or a problem you can help solve, you can actually create a job for yourself. Of course, if the employer is aware of the need or opportunity, all you need to do is let him know that you're the person to handle it.

"I represent an opportunity for you."

"OPPORTUNITY" EXAMPLE— Consider the case of a 28-year-old accountant for a printing company. She decided that if she could find a way to identify small but fast-growing companies, she could contact the presidents and offer to solve a problem that she was sure every one of them had.

The problem was how to find enough time in the day. With her administrative skills, she knew she could lift a lot of time-consuming duties from their shoulders. As it turned out, she was able to identify companies in many industries where presidents responded positively.

One of them admitted he'd known for a full year, in the back of his mind, that he needed someone like her. Until the letter hit his desk, however, he just hadn't taken the time to do something about it. He hired her as his #2 operating person with "full administrative responsibilities."

Take stock of your abilities. Are there certain areas where you're capable of helping almost any firm? If so, you can bring them to the attention of employers in any industry, regardless of whether the kind of position you propose is closely related to your recent experience.

Describe your experience in ways that broaden your appeal

Your previous jobs may have had a narrow focus, and you may be thinking, "I don't have a lot of options." However, here is how you can expand your appeal and uncover more options. Simply make a list of "any experience you've had" in a way that makes the experience and your skills more transferrable.

First, list your experience by your skills and/or your duties that are commonly performed in almost all companies. Identifying your transferrable skills is critical. For example, analyzing, organizing, project management, group presentation skills and problem solving.

Second, list your experience according to various "business functions" that apply to most businesses, such as sales, production, accounting, market research, office administration, etc.

Third, list your experience by using "action verbs" that describe what you did and that translate those things into achievements. For example, controlled, scheduled, systematized, wrote, improved, reshaped, built, created, etc.

The simple fact is, the more different ways you describe your experience, the more it can qualify you for jobs in many career fields and industries. That's because all organizations are basically involved in similar functions. So, before you write your resume, make sure you write out your experience as indicated.

Fourth, you can also take a global or broad view of your experience. This will help you expand the job market possibilities for yourself.

Here's an example of a very simple way to do it. Let's assume that someone is the Manager of Sales Administration for a textbook company that sells to schools in the East.

So that this person might get some new views of themselves, we would first have them draw a small circle. That circle might represent them or others whose jobs could be described in the very same way.

Second, we'd have them draw a slightly larger circle around the first, which would include all of the people who manage sales administration for textbooks, "regardless of where they are sold." Now, when they think of themselves as being part of this group, they realize they can appeal to more firms.

Third, we'd have them draw another, slightly larger circle. It would include all Managers of Sales Administration for "all educational products" (not just textbooks), a still larger group of which they are a part. Once again, the number of potential employers is increased.

A fourth circle? It could include all Managers of Sales Administration for "any products sold to schools" (not just educational products).

Here, the person can appeal to even more employers. We would have the person continue this process, drawing larger circles and figuring out broader job markets for themselves. You might consider going through the same exercise, and then proceed to market yourself to your larger market of potential employers.

With this system you can build appeal beyond your credentials. The key is to design and follow your own communications plan.

First— as part of your plan use words that enhance your appeal

Your need for this can best be appreciated by comparing it to the "platform" of a candidate for the Presidency. The "platform" anticipates questions on major issues by formulating carefully-thought-out position statements to guide the candidate's answers.

Just like a political candidate, you can be perceived as more informed than the next person if you have taken the time to formulate your own communications strategy.

To do this, you must think through your assets, liabilities and goals, and arrive at a formula for guiding communications about yourself. The strategy itself must be geared to maximizing strengths and minimizing liabilities.

Our philosophy revolves around identifying the "core" words and phrases that will be the heart of your communications strategy. This means you want to be ready to use a series of words that communicate your special strengths.

They should become a regular part of "your story" that you communicate to employers, recruiters and others who might be of help.

Please realize that your "tickets alone" (advanced degrees, blue chip background, lofty titles, etc.) will not necessarily motivate any employer to hire you.

Those credentials only offer one form of reassurance that suggests you are right for the job. *This is why you must use words that add interest beyond your credentials.*

Check the words that others in your work or social environment might use to describe you.

- ❑ accurate
- ❑ achiever
- ❑ active
- ❑ adaptable
- ❑ administrator
- ❑ ambitious
- ❑ analytical
- ❑ artistic
- ❑ assertive
- ❑ attentive
- ❑ broad-minded
- ❑ builder
- ❑ calm
- ❑ caring
- ❑ charming
- ❑ compatible
- ❑ competitive
- ❑ conceptual
- ❑ congenial
- ❑ conscientious
- ❑ considerate
- ❑ consistent
- ❑ constructive
- ❑ controller
- ❑ courageous
- ❑ courteous
- ❑ creative
- ❑ cultured
- ❑ decisive
- ❑ demanding
- ❑ dependable
- ❑ designer
- ❑ democratic
- ❑ detailed
- ❑ determined
- ❑ director
- ❑ dignified
- ❑ diplomatic
- ❑ discerning
- ❑ disciplined
- ❑ discreet
- ❑ discriminating
- ❑ driving
- ❑ dynamic
- ❑ economical
- ❑ effective

- ❑ efficient
- ❑ eloquent
- ❑ energetic
- ❑ enterprising
- ❑ enthusiastic
- ❑ esteemed
- ❑ fair
- ❑ flexible
- ❑ forceful
- ❑ forward-thinker
- ❑ frank
- ❑ friendly
- ❑ generous
- ❑ genuine
- ❑ good-natured
- ❑ honest
- ❑ humanitarian
- ❑ imaginative
- ❑ implementer
- ❑ independent
- ❑ individualist
- ❑ initiator
- ❑ innovator
- ❑ inspiring
- ❑ intellectual
- ❑ intense
- ❑ intuitive
- ❑ inventive
- ❑ just
- ❑ keen
- ❑ kind
- ❑ knowledgeable
- ❑ logical
- ❑ loyal
- ❑ manager
- ❑ methodical
- ❑ modest
- ❑ motivator
- ❑ objective
- ❑ observant
- ❑ open-minded
- ❑ opinionated
- ❑ optimistic
- ❑ organizer
- ❑ outgoing
- ❑ outspoken
- ❑ patient

- ❑ perceptive
- ❑ perfectionist
- ❑ persistent
- ❑ personable
- ❑ persuasive
- ❑ punctual
- ❑ planner
- ❑ poised
- ❑ positive
- ❑ practical
- ❑ productive
- ❑ professional
- ❑ punctual
- ❑ quick
- ❑ realistic
- ❑ reliable
- ❑ researcher
- ❑ resourceful
- ❑ responsible
- ❑ respected
- ❑ revitalizer
- ❑ scheduler
- ❑ scientific
- ❑ self-motivated
- ❑ self-reliant
- ❑ sense of humor
- ❑ sensitive
- ❑ shrewd
- ❑ sincere
- ❑ smart
- ❑ sociable
- ❑ sophisticated
- ❑ straightforward
- ❑ strategic
- ❑ supportive
- ❑ systematic
- ❑ tactful
- ❑ tactician
- ❑ talented
- ❑ thinker
- ❑ thorough
- ❑ thoughtful
- ❑ tolerant
- ❑ tough-minded
- ❑ trainer
- ❑ versatile
- ❑ visionary

Second— use key phrases that describe what employers are looking for

When employers recruit people, they usually have a concept in mind— a word description of the kind of person they are looking to hire. In the final analysis, people get hired for the traits, skills and abilities that their own key words and phrases imply.

Decide on some phrases that relate to you, and select those that set you apart from those who are competing with you. For example, you may have "operated effectively under pressure." Perhaps you are "an excellent motivator," or you may have "built a highly effective team."

If you are young and are short on experience, you may be long on personal characteristics. One of your strengths may be that you are "a good listener" or someone who can "work easily with people." A key word or concept can describe a personal characteristic not related to a specific achievement, or it might refer to a particular action or experience.

Most people with five or more years of work experience can make a list of at least twenty key words and concepts. Used appropriately they can set you apart from competition and convey the unique advantages you have to offer.

To take advantage of this opportunity, we need several people who are "results-oriented" and can "work well with all levels of people."

✓ **These are the key traits that employers may be looking for. Make note of those that fit you.**

- ❏ Entrepreneurial strengths
- ❏ Experience with an industry-leading firm
- ❏ Experience in a growth company
- ❏ Resourceful problem-solver
- ❏ Lead by example
- ❏ Intuitive decision-maker
- ❏ An action person
- ❏ Broad-based
- ❏ Formulated policy
- ❏ Ran seminars and conferences
- ❏ Ethics and character of the highest caliber
- ❏ Skillful negotiator
- ❏ Worked closely with top management
- ❏ Practical shirt-sleeve approach
- ❏ Effective in sophisticated environments
- ❏ Work well with people
- ❏ Top management exposure
- ❏ Hard-working achiever/give 100%
- ❏ Made money for the company
- ❏ Ability to get things done
- ❏ Inspire others to better performance
- ❏ Proven record of success
- ❏ Easily win people's confidence
- ❏ Diversified, multi-plant experience
- ❏ Use modern management techniques
- ❏ Make forceful presentations
- ❏ Source of ideas that work
- ❏ Broad administrative skills
- ❏ Reorganized and revitalized
- ❏ Held P&L responsibility
- ❏ Managed a successful operation
- ❏ Unique ability to help others
- ❏ Operations-oriented
- ❏ Willing to try new approaches
- ❏ Bring in-depth technical knowledge
- ❏ Have 10 years plus experience
- ❏ Won the loyalty of those who worked for me
- ❏ Work well alone or as part of a team
- ❏ Quickly cut through non-essentials to the heart of a problem
- ❏ Analyze situations rapidly
- ❏ Meet demanding objectives
- ❏ Initiated sweeping changes
- ❏ Perform against tight deadlines

- ❏ Handle rapid change easily
- ❏ Win cooperation from people at every level
- ❏ Achievements in international operations
- ❏ Know international markets, cultures, etc.
- ❏ Thoroughly familiar with key markets
- ❏ Cut costs without hurting quality
- ❏ Officer and Board member
- ❏ Member of key committees
- ❏ Deliver results, not excuses
- ❏ Set goals/establish controls/follow up and get things done
- ❏ Calm under pressure
- ❏ Bring harmony into situations
- ❏ Have reshaped organizations or departments
- ❏ Effective in short- and long-range planning
- ❏ Versatile troubleshooter
- ❏ Sense of command
- ❏ Turned around marginal operation
- ❏ Consistently find new alternatives
- ❏ Creative flair for putting on events
- ❏ Strong theoretical grounding
- ❏ Extensive community contacts
- ❏ Overhauled ineffective methods
- ❏ Hands-on experience
- ❏ Well-developed instincts for what will sell
- ❏ Personal contacts for attracting business
- ❏ Opened new plants
- ❏ Started prototype operations
- ❏ Salvaged previously unprofitable operations
- ❏ Made many tough decisions
- ❏ Multi-product and multi-market background
- ❏ Sold off undesirable cash-drain properties
- ❏ Brought projects from concept through implementation
- ❏ Precise thinker
- ❏ Not easily intimidated
- ❏ Pay attention to detail

- ❏ Grasp technical matter quickly
- ❏ Simplify complex problems
- ❏ Successfully promote new ideas
- ❏ Establish clear lines of communication
- ❏ Direct meetings skillfully
- ❏ Design new and efficient systems
- ❏ Turned complaints around
- ❏ Effective at dealing with the public
- ❏ Sophisticated
- ❏ Planned fund-raising programs
- ❏ Recruited and trained volunteers
- ❏ Procured major funds and grants
- ❏ Chaired civic or social organizations
- ❏ Know how to structure an organization
- ❏ Use time wisely
- ❏ First hand experience with many cultures
- ❏ Effective moderator and mediator
- ❏ Contributor to educational institutions
- ❏ Effective at organizing labor
- ❏ Focus others' energies toward solutions
- ❏ Bring order out of chaos
- ❏ Build teams who function well in my absence
- ❏ Skilled, versatile writer
- ❏ Bring out creativity in others

- ❏ Diplomatic in difficult situations
- ❏ Function well in rapid-growth situations
- ❏ Veteran of difficult times
- ❏ Participated in a breakthrough
- ❏ Succeeded where others failed
- ❏ Directed start-up
- ❏ Turned around poor attitudes
- ❏ Project management experience
- ❏ High energy level/project enthusiasm
- ❏ Made go/no-go decisions
- ❏ Gained support for new programs
- ❏ Keen observer
- ❏ Good listener
- ❏ Sensitive to others' needs
- ❏ Synthesize diverse ideas
- ❏ Formulate practical action plans
- ❏ Astute researcher
- ❏ Able to set priorities logically
- ❏ Seasoned competitor
- ❏ Effective at dealing with the public
- ❏ Able to direct volunteers
- ❏ Effective at planning conferences
- ❏ Coached winning teams
- ❏ Well-versed in governmental affairs
- ❏ Poised and professional
- ❏ Highly articulate and conversant
- ❏ Special visual and design taste
- ❏ Strong social skills

I am an action person... a problem solver... a skillful negotiator... I can get things done... I am a "team player."

Third— use stories to make your experience sound more interesting

By now you've identified your key strengths and concept phrases. However, while most people who interview you may understand them, they will often forget them in a matter of minutes. In order to ensure that your points are both memorable and credible, use a method for creating interesting stories called the SODAR technique.

SODAR is an acronym which stands for Situation – Opportunities – Duties – Actions – Results. It represents a process of describing your past experience in a way that resembles a motion picture. Here's how you can use it.

S— Situation. Explain a job you held by first describing the situation when you began employment. This enables you to provide some interesting background information, e.g., what had been taking place when you arrived.

O— Opportunities. Then you should integrate into your discussion information about the opportunities that the job seemed to present to you, the group you were part of, and the firm.

D— Duties. Subsequently, you describe your duties.

A— Actions. However, more importantly, your emphasis should quickly move to those actions taken by you and other members of your team.

R— Results. And then relate what results occurred.

SODAR means "telling the whole story." If it's well told it will generate more genuine interest than any recitation of duties or responsibilities. Furthermore, it will help people remember you ahead of others.

Fourth— rehearse your stories before interviews

Many people have said that it was their use of carefully rehearsed **SODAR** stories that most impressed an interviewer and won job offers for them.

This is hardly unexpected. Anyone who has listened to a speech or a sales presentation knows how much more interesting it can be if the speaker uses short stories to demonstrate a point.

Of course, the R in **SODAR** (results) is the most important. Try to quantify the results from the actions taken. For example, you cut costs by $10,000 or 20%. Remember, don't be modest.

In many administrative functions, it is not easy to quantify. In these cases measure results using statements like "I did it in half the time" or "The system I developed was adopted throughout the company" or "I won an award," etc.

For example, a teacher could indicate that student test scores rose, that absenteeism declined or that a waiting list developed for classes. Here are some ideas to guide you in writing about results.

Try to describe results in measures that employers look for, such as dollars, percent increases or units. Indicate any good things you did to help your organizations, and how you took on extra tasks. Describe how you helped your superiors achieve their goals and also the results they achieved.

If you have limited career experience, consider describing accomplishments in college, military service, civic and church activities, or recreational pursuits. Here you can show how you demonstrated either a skill, some special knowledge or a personal quality which might be desirable.

Examples of functions— might include planning and scheduling, recruiting the right person to do a job, or budgeting and controlling expenditures.

Skills— might include diagnosing problems, repairing equipment, writing precise procedures, or researching and analyzing complex information.

Knowledge areas— could be basic chemistry, cost accounting, inventory control, etc.

Personal qualities— which you might have demonstrated could include initiative, resourcefulness and strong drive.

When using a functional skill as a theme, you are transferring your experience "equity" into a new area. For example, planning and scheduling in social matters may be transferable to a people-oriented position in a business organization.

If you are at an early stage in your career and have only a few tangible accomplishments, you could also consider attacking the problem from another point of view. Think about all your positive personal qualities which might make you a desirable candidate. Are you creative? Resourceful? Highly motivated? Persistent?

If you can demonstrate through **SODAR** stories that you possess these traits, you may be preferred over someone else.

Another approach is to use your hobbies to develop a list of knowledge areas which show skills you possess.

For example if you have musical talent, writing ability or are an expert at Chess or Bridge, you may be able to project an image of intelligence. If you are thinking about a major career shift, cite instances where you have faced change before.

Point out how you have rapidly accumulated new knowledge and then delivered results. Show how you thrive on change, how it comes naturally to you, and how you performed in other situations that were new.

Develop **SODAR** stories that cover situations where you can demonstrate the value of fresh thinking as a means to improve productivity or show that you have solved a wide variety of problems in diverse areas.

Now, let's recap all of the primary ways you can expand your marketability. First, broaden your appeal by listing your experience according to (a) business functions, (b) your skills and duties, and (c) your achievements.

Second, since your knowledge and interests are marketable, list all the things you know and any special interests that might appeal to employers.

Remember that your personality, character and enthusiasm are marketable. Since the opportunity you represent is also marketable, list problems you can help an employer solve. Once you have uncovered what's marketable about yourself, build appeal beyond your credentials by making use of a "communications plan. "

Start by identifying words that reflect your special strengths. Then, identify the key phrases which describe your traits, skills and abilities that employers look for. Use them in all your written and verbal communications. However, to make your experiences more interesting and memorable, incorporate them with our **SODAR** story-telling concept.

(For people who are still not sure they have expanded their marketability to its fullest potential, for a very modest cost you can obtain our Career History and Marketability Profile. See page 336.)

Section Two:
How to Get Interviews

Seven topics are covered in Chapters Three through Nine. They include answering ads, using recruiters and selective direct mail marketing. They also review how to identify employers with unadvertised openings, networking, getting employers to create a job, and generating interviews through telemarketing and follow up. Chapter Ten will help you pull all the approaches together as you create your own personal plan of action.

How to Answer Ads for Maximum Results

Using traditional approaches, some people could answer ads forever and still not get the job they really want!

Why answering ads doesn't work well for most people

On a nationwide basis, the sheer number of openings at the executive, managerial and professional level is impressive. However, on a local basis, you may overestimate the importance of the advertised portion of the job market.

Advertised openings represent only 3% of the market!

For example, in the 1990s most estimates place the advertised portion of the job market at only 3% of all openings which get filled. The fact is that less than one in ten employers fills a single professional or managerial job through an ad over a 12-month period. The reason is that most positions are filled privately.

What's more, many of the more attractive advertised openings bring 100, 200, or even 400 responses. Ads which attract up to 1,000 candidates are not that unusual. This clearly makes answering ads the most competitive area you can tackle.

To make things worse, people answer ads without giving any strategic thought to how to gain a competitive advantage. They also use resumes that are average in appearance, disclose far too many liabilities, and fail to highlight why they can fill the advertised position. Rarely interesting or imaginative, they are simply lost among the overwhelming numbers of other candidates.

Answer all attractive ads from the last 13 weeks

Obviously, you should try to gain exposure to as many advertised openings as possible— and you should tailor your message to the requirements of each advertisement.

When you start your search, answer all good ads from the last 13 weeks. This can be a rich source and a quick way to get into action.

A certain percentage of those openings will already be filled, but just as surely, a number will still be open. In some fields, the openings you uncover this way can be quite large. This is especially true as you go for higher income jobs.

Another way to expand your opportunities is to open yourself up geographically. For one or two other geographic areas which you would consider, you should order the Sunday edition of the major newspaper there for a 13 week period.

You can find the names, addresses and phone numbers of those newspapers in your local library, or in the Newspaper Rates and Data publication of Standard Rate & Data Service. By including other geographic areas, you can dramatically increase your potential opportunities.

Delay your answer to every ad and follow up on anything special

As you identify new advertisements to answer, it is usually advisable to delay your response five days, to minimize the risk of not making the first cut.

When employers have to screen a lot of applicants, they begin by discarding any resumes that include anything that will rule the person out. That produces a manageable amount of paperwork which is then reviewed more carefully.

If you respond five days after the ad appears, rather than when the employer was inundated with paper, your chances of getting a good reading go up rather dramatically.

By the way, did you ever see an ad and feel "that describes me exactly?" Well, as a general rule, if you have not heard anything after two weeks have passed, you should follow up. If you were a good fit for the job, answering ads twice can work. Very few of your competitors will do this, and employers give a big edge to people who really want to be with them.

Make use of the downgrade, upgrade and sidegrade strategies

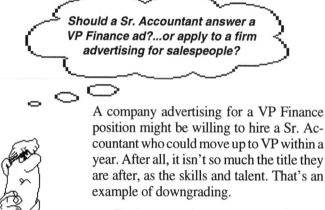

Should a Sr. Accountant answer a VP Finance ad?...or apply to a firm advertising for salespeople?

A company advertising for a VP Finance position might be willing to hire a Sr. Accountant who could move up to VP within a year. After all, it isn't so much the title they are after, as the skills and talent. That's an example of downgrading.

By the same token, a company advertising for a Plant Manager might be persuaded to hire a VP of Manufacturing, provided someone could persuade them such a move would be cost efficient and give added capabilities. That's an upgrade.

Ads can also be used as signals of private openings in other areas of the company. If, for instance, you see a company hiring a number of salespeople, that's a fairly reliable indicator that they are also hiring people in other areas.

Employers tend to go thorough aggressive recruiting in cycles. Any organization that is really expanding its sales force will shortly be looking for support staff as well. This approach can be particularly effective for people at lower levels who see advertised openings for senior-level positions in their field.

Use letters rather than resumes to improve your odds

How do you get more interviews when answering ads? It's very simple. Wherever possible, always use letters rather than resumes.

As I mentioned, because employers receive so many resumes, they tend to start by screening out non-qualifiers. This is a critical point. Since resumes provide more facts, they can work against you in some situations.

Make use of strong letters, ones that are targeted at the requirements for success in the position.

Of course, there are situations where you can use a resume with a cover letter. However, your resume had better be on target for the opening that's being advertised.

Whatever your basis for selecting an advertisement, in your letter be sure to let the employer know just why you selected it. Give a specific reason. Here's a short sample of what I mean.

"I recently read a great article about your firm..."

"Your industry has always fascinated me..."

"In a similar job I not only got results, but I also came in ahead of schedule..."

If you are not getting results, try some innovative approaches

This is important when hundreds of others can also be expected to respond to the same advertisement.

Try getting added information beyond what was in the ad, and then use it in your response. This can be developed by reviewing product literature, annual reports or newspaper articles. Demonstrating industry knowledge works better than anything else.

You might also consider making contact with employees in the company before responding, particularly those who are easiest to befriend: sales and marketing managers, public relations staffers, etc.

Another strategy that can sometimes help involves identifying a reference who is likely to be known to executives of the company, and mentioning his/her name in your correspondence.

The key point to remember is that answering ads is a very competitive arena. If you are not getting the results you want, then some added resourcefulness may be necessary.

Other tips about handling blind ads and money questions

Companies run blind ads to attract employees of competitors, to prevent phone responses, to replace someone on staff, and sometimes to hide a less than attractive reputation. Certain executive recruiters commonly advertise positions in blind ads to keep their assignments confidential.

What do you know? This blind ad sounds just like my job!

Needless to say, you can't really be sure whether or not a blind ad represents a real opportunity, and you can't rule out the possibility that it may be an excellent opportunity. So, if you are not worried about the source of the ad, go ahead and respond.

The one exception is where you suspect it may be your own employer.

Many ads ask you to submit your earnings history. If you are seeking less than $40,000 this is acceptable.

At a higher level, indicate a range or objective, rather than stating your specific current earnings level. As you move past the $60,000 level, avoid disclosure of salary history or objectives. That kind of information is better dealt with during your interviews.

In summary, many people who depend on answering ads get very discouraged about their marketability. One problem involves how they go about it. However, their biggest problem is that they don't seem to realize that answering ads should get less than 10% of their job hunting efforts! To enjoy great success at marketing yourself, you need to be creative, get out of your routine and start using new avenues to find the job you really want.

How to Use Recruiters to Your Best Personal Advantage

The chance of a recruiter filling a job that is just right for you, at the moment you contact them is small.

Improve your odds by contacting large numbers of recruiters with superior materials.

The types of professional recruiters today

The most prestigious category of professional recruiters is the executive search firms that typically fill positions at $60,000 to $250,000 and up. Many people refer to them as executive recruiters or headhunters. Their assignment is to find very qualified candidates who meet highly specialized criteria.

They are retained for searches on an exclusive basis, and most charge their employer clients 30 to 33% of the annual compensation of the position they are seeking to fill. To distinguish themselves within their industry, they are also sometimes referred to as "retainer recruiters."

A second category of recruiters is the professional agencies that are also known as headhunters. These mid-level recruiters usually concentrate on finding people between $30,000 and $85,000 per year and are not normally retained on an exclusive basis. Many of these firms specialize by industry or career function. They are sometimes referred to as "contingency recruiters," in that they only get paid if they fill the position.

When you want to stay in your metropolitan area, many of these professionals can be valuable career allies to professionals and managers. They know what's going on in their local market.

A third category is the traditional employment agencies that focus on clerical and office personnel where incomes are generally lower.

A fourth category is the temporary professional agencies. The newest breed of professional recruiter, they earn fees when employers hire professionals, managers and executives on an interim basis.

Virtually all recruiters work for employers— not job hunters

A key point to remember is that whether they are called search firms, recruiters, headhunters or agencies, all of the firms in these categories work for, and are paid by, employers. Their function is to locate, screen and recommend prospective employees.

This is important for you to understand because some people mistakenly assume that these firms are in business to serve job hunters.

Since mid-level recruiters work on a contingency basis, as a general rule they seek out resumes. While there are many fine firms, if you are employed, you should be cautious about those who may intend to float your resume in the hopes of earning a commission. Executive recruiters work on exclusive assignments and do not depend on "unasked-for resumes."

The job market with recruiters is relatively small

More employers than ever now pay middlemen to do their initial recruiting and pre-employment screening. The number of professional job openings they control is sizable, often estimated at about four times the number of advertised openings, but still only 9% of the market.

Recruiter openings represent only 9% of the market!

If you are an executive, it might also interest you to know that the executive search firms account for fewer than 5,000 placements per month on a national scale. Furthermore, on a national scale fewer than a dozen firms control the majority of the business, even though there are upwards of 600 organizations who claim to be in that segment of the business.

The mid-level recruiters have been playing an increasingly important role in the job market. Besides specializing by industry, many of these firms specialize in accounting, data processing or sales and while some are national franchise organizations, there are many thousands of local firms which can be helpful to you. Like their counterparts in the executive search segment, they are often treated as consultants by employers.

For the most part, recruiters are articulate professionals who have a broad knowledge of business. The successful people in the field are generally excellent marketing executives themselves. While the market they represent is limited, it will pay you to develop relationships with those you respect and to maintain them throughout your career.

How executive recruiters find candidates

For the most part, recruiters have a preference for persons who are achievers, who make a strong first impression and who are successfully employed in other firms. These are the individuals who are most presentable to their clients and who are easiest to sell to them.

Their sources for finding people range from directories and articles in the press, to their own contacts and files of resumes.

The best relationships with these firms are the ones that begin with their contacting you. Being visible in your industry is the major key to success with recruiters. Being in a hot field or industry can improve things still further.

If you have been writing articles, giving speeches, or receiving awards, you have probably been contacted by some of these firms. If you have kept track of the recruiters that have called you, one of the first things you should now do is renew these relationships.

Executive recruiting in the 1990s

It is important to understand that while recruiters do not work for you, they can be very helpful to your campaign. When they are retained by a corporation for a search, recruiters will often help management determine the type of individual they are looking for, and they may even play a primary role in setting up job specifications. This consulting role is one of the reasons why leading firms command substantial fees.

Most of the top search firms are respected companies with well-earned reputations. They have recruited many of the business leaders in both the U.S. and Europe. While many leading executive search firms are headquartered in New York, Chicago and Los Angeles, they receive assignments from throughout the U.S. and the world. Some of them are divisions of consulting firms or CPA firms which offer search as an auxiliary service.

Certain recruiters enjoy considerable prestige, often working only on select high-level assignments. However, there are also many very fine smaller firms who specialize in just a single industry or several industries or disciplines.

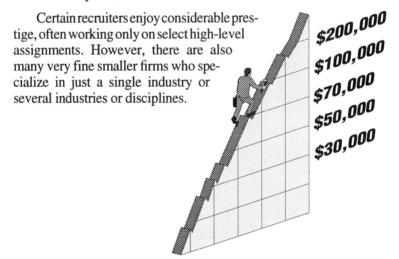

$200,000

$100,000

$70,000

$50,000

$30,000

Finding the right recruiters— and making your contact by direct mail

Some people can obtain the personal names of recruiters from friends and other job seekers. They then contact these people and mention that their associates suggested they call. However, getting through by phone is difficult unless you leave the name of your organization, and they think you might be a source of business. What's more, they are still going to ask you to simply send them a resume.

You can also find recruiters in the Yellow Pages and via directories which are advertised in the classifieds. Princeton/Masters also makes available low-cost computer generated reports on all levels of recruiters with names, addresses and specialties. See page 336 for more information.

To get results through a mail campaign, you are going to have to send them a superior summary of your qualifications. At an executive level, consider mailings of 300 or more. Keep in mind that recruiters are "assignment" oriented. They work on active contracts and will have only secondary interest in people from other specialties.

Using impressive materials, positive response usually ranges from 1% to 4% over a six-week period— depending on your field, industry and income level. If your correspondence fails to supply a phone number that is answered during normal business hours, you will lose a lot of leads. Voice mail service or an answering machine is a must. Another point to remember is that a second mailing to the same list three months later usually produces equal results.

Regardless, recruiters will be primarily interested in those viewed as marketable, who have blue chip or high-demand backgrounds, and who have industry knowledge that can quickly help their clients.

Sell yourself to recruiters with these tips in mind

Get to know as many as you can before you need them. Be honest while pursuing a soft sell. If you are desperate or too available, they will never recommend you to their clients.

❏

Initiate major recruiter contact soon after the beginning of your campaign. Because timing is critical, "luck" can play a significant role. Your chances of reaching recruiters when they have an assignment for your specific background may be slim, and career changers can't expect much here.

❏

Many large firms are contacted by 50 to 200 job seekers each day. This means there will be instances where a recruiter calls you *months* after the firm first receives your resume.

❏

You will be most popular with recruiters if you are a person who will explore more attractive situations but who is not too unhappy with his or her current employer.

❏

If you are highly marketable, some recruiters may want to send your credentials to a number of employers under their letterhead. *That may not be in your best interest.*

❏

While recruiters always prefer to have full information at their disposal, early disclosure of financial information is unprofessional and makes people seem too available. In the future maintain a high profile in your career field— one which makes you as visible as possible.

In summary, recruiters can be very important, especially for young and middle-income professionals. However, many people depend far too much on them, with the result that job hunting becomes a waiting game. Subsequently, a high percentage get discouraged about their marketability and draw negative conclusions about the job market. No more than 10% of your job hunting efforts should be directed toward recruiters.

How to Get Interviews by Selective Direct Mail Marketing

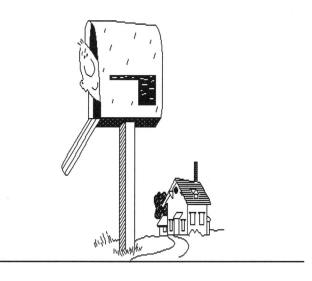

Large scale, but highly selective direct mail, as well as small custom mailings, are both integral parts of this system. They are often the easiest and fastest way to find the right new job.

A fast way to get the right interviews

To make direct mail work, you need superior resumes and letters along with just the right selection of organizations and people to contact. What's more, you need to understand how to use telemarketing in conjunction with direct mail.

Without all of the above, any mailings can be a waste of time. Even then, it is a sophisticated and low-percentage response game. The key is to follow traditional direct marketing and follow-up techniques. Here are some initial thoughts for you to consider.

❏ Direct mail marketing works well because you can reach your largest possible number of potential buyers. You can project your best image, avoid initial disclosure of any liabilities, and make independent contact that is free from competition. What's more, you have a whole universe of possibilities to contact.

❏ This method for generating interviews also offers the best potential for helping you change careers or land a position at a significant increase in earnings.

❏ Direct mail marketing is easier than ever with the recent revolution that has taken place in personal computers and databases.

Finding the right employers to contact — deciding on your priority list

The first thing you need to do is draw up a highly selective list of your preferred organizations and people in them to contact. And, as we already said, don't make the mistake of ruling out businesses with less than 100 employees. These organizations reach hiring decisions fast. The key is to join one that is in a growth industry.

Your "priority list" needs to be developed according to the industries you are best suited for, your preferred locations, and by the size of organization that is most appropriate for you. The people you will want to contact should be a level or two above where you want to be.

In large organizations senior vice presidents in charge of specific functions are recommended targets for most professionals. In smaller firms you will need to reach the one or two top executives or owners.

To assemble your list you will want to draw upon computer databases to save yourself both time and money. This is really essential as a time-saver. Instead of spending time in the library, it's really the best way to go. Be sure to see pages 327 and 328 for database services.

Your next step is to divide your initial list into three parts by identifying your "best of best," other prime choices, and those who are really secondary choices you might consider.

This carefully tailored target list of employers should be added to as you go through your search. Your goal, of course, is to get an interview with the right person in these organizations. To do that, you can also draw upon our telemarketing and networking advice. However, this discussion will be focused on direct mail marketing.

Start with an initial large "macro" marketing effort to your priority list

Normally the first step of your action plan should call for large mailings to selected targets. I call it your "macro" mailing. Your goal is to get your credentials into the hands of as many of these employers as possible.

The assumption is that among the careful list you have put together there is a demand for your talents in the marketplace, and a small percentage of your targets will probably be looking for someone like you either right now or over the next few months.

Here, a superior presentation of your background and what you can do for the company are key. For those with highly marketable backgrounds and skills, your large mailing effort alone may generate more than enough interview activity. If it doesn't produce, it is a sign your materials were off base or your background and list selection did not fit.

Of course, the higher your income objective, the larger the effort that is necessary. This is because direct mail campaigns only generate a small percentage of interviews. Everything depends on proper targets and superior materials.

There are certain specialties in which job seekers have a limited number of potential employers. For example: musicians, educators, broadcasters, airline pilots, etc. Here, your campaign will be most effective if it is based upon relatively long letters.

Design a small "custom" mailing to the best of your priority list

About four weeks after your macro marketing effort, your next step will involve sending a highly customized marketing letter directed toward a smaller number of companies who are your very best prospects.

Depending on the size of your list, this effort might be restricted to your best of best. Typically, here you are talking about no more than 15% to 20% of your entire priority list.

Here, through added knowledge or research, you must communicate something in your letter that customizes your approach to each employer. In essence, you need to insert a few thoughts or paragraphs which create a more tailored marketing approach.

By the way, the same employers contacted in the initial macro stage can be contacted again in the micro phase without doing any harm whatsoever to the effectiveness of either effort. However, it is wise to vary your materials. If at first you sent a cover letter with a two-page resume, now you should use a two-page letter without a resume, or with a resume that has a different appearance.

The custom approach relies on more personally tailored communications that take more time and always merit phone follow-up. The targets are approached over a longer period, so you can afford to take the extra time to personally call everyone you have written. Nevertheless, for most senior executives a plan for at least 200 or more custom mailings is essential. In most cases, two-page letters *(without a resume attached)* produce the best results.

Success depends on your list and your phone work— as well as your materials

Let's assume you were seeking a sales manager's position. Here are some of the direct mail actions you might consider taking.

1—High risk

Sent to CEOs regardless of your level, functional area or geography. Takes a minor miracle to work today.

2—Slightly better... may result in no response   ★

Sent to firms and people by generic titles, e.g. all VPs of Sales at Fortune 500 firms. Takes great credentials to work.

3—Much better... can do very well for many people   ★★

Sent to VP Sales, by personal name, selected by industry, size and location. Can be very good with telephone follow-up.

4—Very, very good... works very well   ★★★

Sent to VP Sales by name, in industries where you have experience, mention it early, and follow up on the phone.

5—Excellent...   ★★★1/2

Sent to VP Sales you have spoken to first on the phone. Great if you can get your telemarketing on a roll.

6—Also Excellent... if you can arrange it   ★★★★

Sent to VP Sales, by name, where mailing goes out under someone else's letterhead and title.

7—Outstanding... you can probably do some   ★★★★1/2

Sent to VP Sales, by name, to whom you've been referred by someone you can mention in your letter, with telephone follow up.

8—Best: only champion networkers can do it!   ★★★★★

Sent to VP Sales, by name, that you have met on some occasion, either social or business, with telephone follow-up.

There are four popular forms of direct marketing letters

✔ **Cover Letters**

✔ **Letter Resumes**

✔ **Third-Party Letters**

✔ **Hand- written memos**

Cover letters should be interesting and brief. Since your resume will be attached, the cover letter will be the first thing the reader sees. Make sure it's good.

Letter resumes are stand-alone letters which are not forwarded with a resume. They should provide sufficient "resume-type information" to stimulate interest. Use the letter-resume whenever you want to fully tailor the description of your credentials, and avoid revealing any liabilities.

Third-party letters can be enormously effective if the right person is writing on your behalf.

Handwritten memos are fast and easy to get out, and executives are used to such notes. If you have a superior resume which is right-on- target for your audience, attaching such notes can work very well.

Obviously, the content of your letters will be critically important. Materials that emphasize what you can do and the results you can bring are ideal. Next best are letters that talk about some of your previous accomplishments and the results of those contributions. Least effective are letters that simply list your past experience and work history.

Letter writing is easier if you think of it in three basic parts

Some people start without a clear picture of what they intend to say, then get caught up in telling their story, and wind up with a highly disorganized letter. To avoid this trap, think of your letter copy in three parts: the opening, the body and the closing sections.

The Opening — should demonstrate your specific interest (knowledge of the firm, its industry, etc.) and explain your reason for writing. Here is a sample. *After learning of your company's expansion into several new markets, I decided to contact you about what I could contribute.*

The Body — must convey your qualifications and potential benefits for the reader. You should lead off with your best selling points. Enlarge upon them, citing examples when appropriate, and present yourself as the answer to a need or problem. Here is sample body copy:

When I arrived at Software, Inc., the $12 million company was experiencing slow growth. It was apparent that the firm had two major needs: new business and a successful new product introduction. Here's how I filled those roles: Personally sold over $4 million to new accounts, including investment banks, commercial banks and other financial institutions. At the same time I hired 5 effective managers, each of whom has been instrumental in helping our new product line exceed expectations.

The Closing — should be straightforward. It should restate your interest and confirm your desire for an interview. Here is a sample closing.

The opportunity to join your company would be of great interest. As you can see, my background includes many accomplishments in your industry. I will phone you next week to arrange a personal meeting.

To get your best results, follow these direct marketing rules

Direct mail marketing is a separate marketing specialty. What works and what doesn't has already been proven!

❏ Long copy works best. Don't be afraid of long letters if they are crisp.

❏ A mailing to individuals by name is the only way to go.

❏ The look of your material must be clean and professional.

❏ A handwritten envelope marked "private" or "personal" will always out-perform a standard mailing.

❏ Keep your sentences short and simple. Avoid flowery words; be direct and to the point.

❏ Keep the paragraphs short— no more than five or six lines. Indent the first line of each paragraph.

❏ Sign your name with a blue felt tip pen. It implies forcefulness and generates response. If you write a handwritten P.S., it will almost always be read, so make the copy good.

❏ Don't hard sell. Overselling is as bad as underselling. "If this guy is so good, why does he try so hard?"

❏ Never begin a letter by asking for a job. Also, avoid use of the term "job hunting," and stress career orientation.

❏ A good technique when writing to a stranger is to say you have some "ideas" or "knowledge" that can benefit the firm. Then, offer to share the knowledge in a meeting.

❏ If you have industry experience, mention it early! There is nothing quite like an industry hook.

❑ Use the names of both the firm and the individual in the body of your letter. Also, sign letters with your full name— never use initials.

❑ In most cases don't try to explain "why" you are looking.

❑ Persuasive letters are alive and enthusiastic, as well as personal and warm. They "read" just like you "speak."

❑ When you've written a letter, read it out loud. If you find you are changing parts as you read, it needs more work.

❑ Personalize your correspondence. Your letters will seem warmer if you use pronouns such as "I," "my," or "we."

❑ Always be enthusiastic. Everyone prefers people who really want to be associated with them.

❑ Pay careful attention to editing. Eliminating extraneous information will make the important facts stand out.

❑ If you are addressing influential people, recognize their position in a complimentary manner and explain your situation briefly.

❑ Making use of a third party can be very effective. You do not have to be a close friend to ask for third-party assistance. Just make it easy for the third party to assist. Offer to prepare a letter for their signature and be sure they are knowledgeable about your situation.

❏ Commit yourself to a telephone follow up. Name the date and general time when you will call.

❏ After every interview you should quickly write a follow-up letter. It should show continued enthusiasm for the company and/or the position.

❏ Never mention your expected income.

❏ With very few exceptions, your letters should be single spaced with double spaces between paragraphs.

❏ With the exception of holiday weekends, the best day to mail is Sunday. This way you will normally reach people between Tuesday and Thursday, which is the time they are most likely to be at their desks.

❏ Avoid mailings between Thanksgiving and Christmas. Summer mailings also yield less than average results.

❏ Keep exact records of all of your direct mail, and keep everything you receive back— including rejections. If you do a follow-up mailing, experience indicates you will get 80% of the response generated from your first mailing.

❏ You may also want to consider using telegrams and special delivery. Telegrams are always read. Faxing unasked-for resumes is a waste of time.

❏ If you have a strong interest in a particular employer, you should consider sending materials to as many as five individuals in a large organization.

The response you can expect from your direct mail marketing effort

The lower your position objectives, the higher the response you can expect from your mailing. Here are some criteria developed from large-scale and well-designed mailings to *local area employers* in business occupations of average demand.

❏ Under $40,000, you should look for a 3% to 4% positive response.

❏ In the $40,000 to $60,000 range, a 2% to 3% positive response is good.

❏ Above the $60,000 level, a 1% positive response is good.

❏ Above the $100,000 level, a 0.5% positive response is good.

Positive response refers to any favorable inquiry over a 4 to 6 week period. It may be a request for further information, a phone discussion or a request for an interview.

For example, assume you are at $80,000 and that you have done a mailing to 1,000 firms within a couple of hours of where you live.

If over a period of 4 to 6 weeks, and as a result of both your marketing and follow up, 8 to 12 firms (1 to 1.5%) express an interest in a meeting, you will have done well. Remember these will usually be your best possible leads— where employers are responding with a specific need in mind right now. Effective use of the phone is the key to achieving any dramatic improvement in these statistics.

Notes for executives on direct marketing, long copy and pre-selling

I'm often amused by executives who say that direct mail marketing doesn't work. You've seen horror stories about unemployed executives who have sent out 5,000 resumes— who have yet to get an interview— and therefore things are really tough out there!

Well, obviously, if you can't come up with a good, well-written story and the right mailing list, then anything is possible. However, most executives can achieve far more with direct mail than they thought possible. It takes excellent writing, the right targets, telephone follow-up and adherence to proven rules of direct mail. But considering your career is at stake, it's worth it.

Every day we are all on the receiving end of direct mail. However bad that junk mail may look to you, the fact is that the ones you see again and again are working; otherwise companies wouldn't be wasting money by repeating the process.

Direct mail is a game of testing, revising and testing some more, until you get the right return for the right dollars. And, perhaps the number one rule in direct mail is that "long copy is the name of the game," because that's what it takes to motivate all of us to action from *unasked-for correspondence.*

Why? Well, give it a little thought. Let's assume your local lawn mower shop wants you to come in a see a new product they are carrying. Furthermore, assume that you and your next door neighbor are both out cutting your lawns on a brutally hot day. However, your lawn mower keeps sputtering and coughing, stopping and starting, and finally it passes out completely.

Then, the postman arrives at both residences with this long piece of junk mail that tells you all about a revolutionary new lawn mower, a long explanation of why it's superior to every-thing else ever manufactured and guess what it's available locally. Now, chances are your neighbor will look at the mailing piece for about two seconds and toss it, wondering how anyone could ever read all that material.

Obviously, he isn't in the market for a lawn mower. On the other hand, because the mailing piece has reached you at precisely the right time, you are apt to read it quite thoroughly. Perhaps you might be motivated to a local visit and a purchase!

Now, your position relative to using direct mail is really very similar. Your interest is in reaching the right person at an employer who might be in the market for someone like you right now. No one else counts. That is your number one goal!

What are the chances? Well, it's a low percentage game. However, if you have the right targets and a good story, then those few you reach who are in the market for someone like you are going to want to read about you! After all, they have a problem to be solved or an opportunity to be capitalized on!

For senior executives, an initial mailing campaign of 1,000 or more is usually recommended. This "macro marketing" effort can include all three levels of your priority list. Typically, you would make use of either a cover letter and a two-page resume, or a two-page letter that could be adjusted for different industries. Mailings in waves are suggested to allow time for telephone follow-up.

For six-figure executives who are marketable on a national scale, initial mailings of 3,500 are not uncommon. Total cost from research and resume distribution services average $2.00 per contact, including the cost of research, individual letter and envelope typing, printing of resumes and signing, folding, stuffing, sealing and stamping.

Direct mail and telemarketing have to work together to produce the optimum results. For small custom mailings, I would go for a handwritten envelope marked "private and confidential," sent with a regular postage stamp. By the way, the job of the letter itself would not only be to produce an interview, but to pre-sell you. Then, when you meet, hopefully the process has been moved downstream a step.

Executive Case Histories

■ **At $60,000.** Our first example involves a client who had a very narrow objective. A $60,000 financial analyst in Boston, this person wanted to return to Rochester.

The problem was he would only consider joining either Kodak or Xerox who both had a major presence there. To get the results we wanted, we came up with a plan to contact 22 different people on a staggered basis. The contacts ranged from board members to people who would be my client's peers.

Twelve contacts were made before we could get the two interviews we wanted, and within five weeks we had one offer on the table. The point for relating this particular story is to caution you against a direct mail mistake made by 95% of the public. Typically, they send off a cover letter and resume, but when they get their first rejection letter they give up.

■ **At $100,000+.** Another situation involved a close friend and sales manager in the photo industry. He knew that a Japanese camera manufacturer was going to set up its own sales operation in the U.S. This gentleman had the ideal qualifications to head up their operations.

Our marketing approach in this case was to first approach someone who personally knew the founder of the Japanese firm and who would pass on the private direct mail correspondence we developed. That was the only way to be sure it would be read!

To find the proper individual and gain his support took us several weeks. We then made use of a four-page letter that was written several times in English, which was then translated into Japanese, only to be revised several more times. The introduction worked and after four meetings in New York and Tokyo, negotiations were completed.

■ **At $250,000+.** This example of direct mail involved two men simultaneously — the EVP and number two man in a New Jersey pharmaceutical firm and the President of the consumer products division of the same firm. Both were terminated as a result of a merger, and both were caught by surprise.

The EVP was moved into a Presidency with a major division of another pharmaceutical firm in NY inside of 10 weeks. Less than 80 three-page custom letters were circulated within the industry— each of which was followed up by our client.

The other executive campaigned for 18 weeks before relocating as CEO of a smaller West Coast firm in consumer durable products. Fifteen hundred letters were involved, and we made use of two different three-page biographies. This gentleman has since built the firm into a multi-billion dollar business.

■ **At $500,000+.** Another example involved the CEO of a Fortune 500 firm who was ousted by his Board of Directors. When we took on the assignment to help market this gentleman, it appeared loaded with problems. He insisted on not using any of his own substantial contacts and would not contact any recruiters or employers directly himself.

This left us with the need to launch a third-party direct mail and telemarketing effort. The campaign took nine months and involved hundreds of phone calls, along with 7,500 contacts by direct mail. They went out under the names of three different third-party sponsors. The materials involved two-page letters and three different biographies we created. Each of the bios had different slants on our client's experience. The results brought three attractive offers: CEO of a division of a large firm, Dean of a graduate business school, and Executive VP for a growth firm.

In summary, some people may tell you that direct mail marketing doesn't work. However, they probably did a job search without understanding that direct marketing is the most scientific area of sales and marketing and without having the benefit of the advice just discussed. If you distribute ordinary materials, use the wrong list, have false expectations or ignore the rules, you will be wasting your time. However, use our direct mail and telemarketing formula and that may be all you need.

How to Find Employers With Unadvertised Job Openings

These events are the keys
to finding private openings.
❏ new products
❏ firms relocating
❏ new leases
❏ higher sales & profits
❏ new officers
❏ planned expansions

Why most jobs are filled privately

Most jobs are filled by referrals, from resumes on file, or through people who contact firms at the right time.

This discussion is about gaining access to private job openings. Many studies have indicated that about 85% of all openings are filled privately. How do companies do this? Well, they seek to fill openings privately by looking first within their own companies. They may also review any resumes they've kept on file.

But in most cases, they will ultimately fill their positions through personal referrals or by hiring someone who simply contacts them at the right time. By hiring in this manner, organizations avoid the substantial costs of recruiter fees and advertising expenses.

Now, if you can learn where these openings exist, it stands to reason that you can have a major edge over your competitors. What's more, you might be able to have your credentials up for singular consideration, instead of applying right along with scores of others. To find employers with unadvertised openings, all you need to do is follow events in the press. We call those situations Spot Opportunities.

To find spot opportunities just read the business press

You can uncover jobs which are not advertised through mailings, telemarketing and networking, but the most direct way is simple.

Events occur every day in thousands of firms that ultimately lead managers to begin the process of privately looking for new people. These events are often reported in local and national business publications, trade magazines, newsletters and newspapers.

There you will find articles on growth situations, new divisions, new facilities, new products, reorganizations, acquisitions, high-level executive changes, and plans for investments or expansion.

For companies undergoing these transitions, chances are they will need to attract good people to handle problems or capitalize on their opportunities. The activity in these companies won't usually be limited to one or two functions either. They can be expected to need people in all functional categories— sales, marketing, finance, etc.

While private openings are being filled by all types of employers, they are filled with far greater frequency in organizations experiencing significant change.

Use "ripple-effect thinking" to pinpoint opportunities

When you read about a company that is giving out signals that they may be hiring at an above-average rate, don't stop at the obvious implications. Use what we refer to as "ripple-effect thinking." This is simply taking the time to think about all of the changes that may be occurring in the company— up and down the line and across many functions.

You may also get some good ideas about using information that you read about one company— to find opportunities with a company's suppliers, customers and even their competitors. To take full advantage of spot opportunities, consider the following example.

New product or new divisions— the obvious spot opportunity

You read that a manufacturer is starting a division to sell a revolutionary kind of stapler— one that is appropriate for use in packaging where health requirements now prevent use of ordinary staplers.

The obvious implications are that this company could very well need people in marketing and sales. Since it's a new division, you might also expect that there will be some need for finance people as well.

If you're a packaging engineer, you might also project a need for that capability to support the sales effort. Those possibilities would be real enough, but now let's use "ripple-effect thinking" to see if we can infer some other needs.

Ripple effect— with competitors

If you're an engineer with knowledge in this product area, you know this concept will be of concern to competitors. You might contact them to help in the new product area.

Ripple effect— on customers of the company

Or, you may be someone who is experienced in dealing with regulatory authorities. You recognize that the potential customers for this product will have to deal with these authorities to gain product approval. Consequently, this firm might need someone like you to take charge of regulatory matters.

Ripple effect— when career changing

Consider the case of an executive who had been an executive director with a charity and a fund-raiser for a university. For a number of reasons, he wanted to make a move to the corporate sector. "Ripple-effect thinking" helped him to uncover a number of attractive possibilities.

He learned that a major corporation was expanding its nuclear fuel facilities. He reasoned that the company would have to deal with community groups opposing these facilities. Given his experience in community affairs and controversial subjects, he wrote the company about whether they might have an opening for someone to fill that need.

In another instance, he learned about a manufacturer where sales were declining in their major lines. They were shifting emphasis to another product line— expensive medical equipment sold to hospitals. He was familiar with hospitals and the problems they faced with raising money. He saw that this company would be more successful if they had someone who could work with potential hospital customers, showing them how to raise funds for this equipment.

Don't ignore firms with problems

Reorganizations involve shifts within the executive ranks. They usually spell opportunity for those who are at the next lower level, and then changes ripple through the organization down through the line.

Problems often imply one of two things: managers in certain functions haven't been performing well, or the company needs to develop new capabilities in order to survive and grow. Organizations with problems often need help from the following types of people:

❑ Marketing people who can identify new markets and find new applications for existing products.

❑ Sales people who can increase volume.

❑ Applications engineers who can design and develop new products and applications for existing products.

❑ Financial executives who can cut costs or raise capital.

❑ Manufacturing people who can find more cost-efficient ways to produce goods and reduce overhead.

❑ Skilled negotiators who can win more favorable terms with labor, suppliers and customers.

❑ Real estate and financial people who can redeploy assets or dispose of unwanted facilities.

❑ General managers who can take total responsibility for plant closings, consolidations and streamlinings.

❑ CEOs and COOs who can supply new leadership.

❑ Human resource executives who can help find all these other people, while directing outplacement activities with certain parts of the work force.

Who to contact in growth companies of interest

If you are seeking a position as a senior executive, the CEO or a board member will often be the logical person for you to contact. For positions below senior level, other targets will normally be preferred. The human resources manager may be aware of most openings in a company. However, the VP of your major function is going to be a better alternative.

Keep in mind that many employers undergoing major change are actually the smaller and faster growing firms, and they are far less constrained by hiring traditions common to major companies.

In the case of many growth companies, the force for their continued growth may rest with their willingness to gamble on people without industry experience and without all the answers. Most companies on a fast-track are looking for individuals with the best natural ability and for people who also have enthusiasm, dedication and a willingness to work hard.

Assuming you have marketable talents, a straightforward message which makes clear how you can contribute is likely to stimulate interest.

Using the spot opportunity process has been the key to success for people at all levels and from all occupations. On the following page are a few examples.

Here's how a few people have capitalized on private openings

❑ In one instance, a product manager learned about a company which grew at over 100% for each of the past four years. He called the Vice President of Marketing and within three weeks received an attractive job offer at a base of $57,000.

❑ A financial executive learned that a troubled manufacturer was divesting a division to raise cash. He called the new president and arranged to meet him and explain how he might help. Four weeks later he became the CFO of this company.

❑ A homemaker learned that a major firm was establishing a warehouse in the next town. She phoned to learn the name of the person responsible and was the first administrator hired.

❑ A marketing manager read that a European corporation had bought a local company. He wrote to express interest and suggested a dialogue when European officials visited there. Twelve weeks later, he was VP-Marketing, U.S.A at $120,000.

❑ An assistant plant manager learned about the financial troubles of a small firm. He wrote to the EVP, explaining that he had turned around a similar operation in less than six months. The results: three meetings with officials followed by a job offer as Plant Manager at $38,000.

❑ An ambitious sales manager read that a leading firm in his industry had recently acquired two other companies in the field and planned to implement a major market expansion. Sensing that this would soon create a need for high-powered sales executives, he placed a phone call, and four weeks later he was offered a VP Sales position at $56,000.

In summary, it's been often said that information is power, and that's exactly what spot opportunities provide. The ability to recognize and go after opportunity has been critical to the success of many people. It is especially important for those who want to change careers or industries.

How to Use Networking to Get the Right Referrals

Networking involves getting others to:

❑ act as a reference
❑ suggest referrals
❑ contact employers
❑ recommend recruiters
❑ supply information
❑ make introductions

Focused networking is easier than you think

Networking is the most recommended way to get a new job. It is essential because it can dramatically increase your contacts and your chances for finding out about unadvertised jobs.

Networking involves establishing and using contacts to assist in your job search. By networking effectively, your phone presence, personality and follow-through can substitute for a lack of the right experience. Your network can simply be a group of contacts who provide helpful information. This can include information such as positions available, companies in a hiring mode, or names of other people who can provide similar information.

There is a big difference between focused networking which is clearly targeted by industry or involves influentials, and universal networking, which may be purely social or for advice purposes. The latter can take a long time.

Networking works because every organization experiences turnover— and a lot more of it than they like to admit. That's why jobs are available with far more organizations over the course of a year than most people realize.

Focused networking has to do with quickly finding specific industry people who can offer you a job. Networking within a specific industry where you have experience or interests and networking efforts directed to influential people are core parts of the Princeton/Masters system.

While this chapter will review a broad base of potential networking actions, those are the two that will most likely merit some action on your part. Even if you don't plan to change jobs again in the foreseeable future, start collecting business cards and keep your rolodex up to date. It works!

Networking— An approach for almost everyone

I've gathered the top 1% of my network here today...

The greater the number of people in your network, the greater your access to other groups. Contacts may include former employers, suppliers, business associates, priests, rabbis, ministers, alumni, community contacts, insurance agents, bankers, merchants, friends, relatives, teachers, trade association officers, attorneys, clients, etc.

People often think that their existing contacts will make job hunting easy. This rarely turns out to be true. Let your campaign get under way with other approaches. If you are like most people, you may refine your goals.

Pyramiding refers to capitalizing on the name of one individual to gain an interview with another. For example, if you were meeting with one firm, and you felt that the interview would not be productive, you could lead into a discussion about another firm. You would then ask your interviewer whether or not he felt that it would be a firm for you to explore. He's likely to routinely say, *"Of course, you ought to contact them."* Next you would write the president of the new firm something like the following, *"In my recent meeting with Mr. X, he suggested that it might be of value if I arranged to speak with you."*

Networking—
Through influential people

Here is an example. A young executive from Boston wanted to relocate to Seattle. Unfortunately, she had no connections there. She launched a direct mail and follow-up telephone campaign, and within ten days she was able to generate six interviews from referrals provided by board members of three banks.

Governors, congressmen, state senators and politicians at almost any level can be excellent sources for referrals. The same is true for prominent doctors and lawyers who speak with many people during the course of each day.

Clergymen, accountants, hospital trustees, members of the Chamber of Commerce or other civic groups, members of industrial development boards, investment bankers, insurance brokers, and many others also fall into this category.

Younger people should think of an influential as anyone who might have some influence on your obtaining a job offer. For example, if you were an engineer interested in a particular firm, you could call and ask to be connected to the engineering department.

You could then explain your situation to the person who answers, and ask for a referral to someone who would take a few minutes to speak with you. Most people are eager to help others, and it is surprisingly easy to develop a network of contacts you have not previously known.

Networking—
Through business activities

You can expand your business network by dining in restaurants patronized by those in your field, or attending seminars, parties and supplier meetings. Anything you can do to gain visibility will result in easier initiation of new contacts. Taking an active role in community affairs, politics and service clubs, along with speaking at seminars and trade associations, will serve as a means of accomplishing the same end.

Here's an example: *A woman was relocated from Philadelphia to Lake Forest, Illinois, because of her husband's promotion. After arriving, she volunteered to work in the campaign of an executive who was a candidate for Town Council. In the next six weeks, she met many people who offered to introduce her to people they knew. She made use of these introductions and it wasn't long before she was in the best position she had ever had.*

Trade shows can be an efficient medium for developing contacts. In one location you usually have dozens of people assembled, and all of them are there because they want to talk to people.

One imaginative sales manager visited each of the major hotels where conventioneers were staying. He met dozens of people in both hotel lobbies and hospitality suites. As it turned out, the informal atmosphere paved the way for his development of contacts with those who could help him. Within days he had lined up all the interviews he needed.

Networking—
Through associations

Many professional organizations, alumni and trade associations act as intermediaries between job hunters and employers.

Most groups operate as "resume clearing houses." In general, professional organizations are most effective for young people, particularly young graduates who are specialists seeking under $35,000.

The executive directors of associations, Chambers of Commerce, and fraternal organizations such as the Toastmasters International or Jaycees usually have many "lines" into their communities. They know where growth is occurring.

Professional groups also fund and manage business magazines, journals, newsletters, memberships lists, industry directories, trade show catalogs and many other publications. The editors at these journals can be influential contacts.

Exhibitor directories at trade shows can provide a list of firms in a given field and provide names of people to contact. *The Encyclopedia of Associations* is a source for the names and addresses of thousands of these organizations.

Networking— Through advice letters

We don't advise this for professionals, managers or executives. However, if you are at a junior level or seeking your first civilian job, you may wish to encourage suggestions from senior executives concerning the direction of your career.

You could even consider seeking advice by writing top executives with whom you are not personally acquainted.

Of course, your "advice letter" would have to be well phrased. You must convey your respect for their authority and expertise on these matters in an appealing way.

The object of this approach is to have them take more than a passing interest in your success. During any discussions you should also lay the groundwork for additional phone contact during your job search. Your goal would be to obtain job leads in either the firms of these executives or those of their associates.

Networking—
From a zero base

Many professionals have pointed out that it is not really difficult to make totally new acquaintances starting from a zero base. A technique for doing this is what is commonly called the "insider approach."

Take the case of a young woman interested in working for a photocopy company. She could call a salesperson and ask, "Is there a chance you could help me?" She could then ask the person to spend a few minutes to give her an estimate of her chances for getting into the firm.

Once a first meeting is accomplished, it's easy to get a third-party introduction to a person who might be responsible for recruitment. By the way, the person contacted doesn't have to be a salesperson. It can be an engineer, an advertising manager or anyone who might be a decision-maker at your level of interest.

For many people, starting with an existing employee is an easy way to get in the door if you think an opening is likely to exist. This "insider approach" has also worked for more advanced professionals as well.

It is important that you ask the right questions

When probing for information from someone you don't know well, keep the questions broad, asking about the industry. In general, such inquiries are less apt to make the person wonder whether you are "fishing" for a position right then and there.

If you requested a meeting for information and try to turn it into a job interview, it will look like you got through the door on false pretenses.

Naturally, you want to know about trends in any business you might work in. So, questions like the ones that follow are suitable to ask of people whom you have only just met. They can facilitate the kind of shop talk shared at a trade conference.

Here are some sample questions you might consider asking for general information:

❑ *What are some important long-term trends affecting your industry?*

❑ *With those trends in mind, what skills and expertise are companies apt to be looking for in new people?*

❑ *What are some good sources of additional information— either articles and reports, or people to talk to?*

❑ *Who are the recruiters active in the industry?*

❑ *If I ever get a position in (the department you are interested in), are people in that area really valued in the company, or are they off in a corner?*

❏ *What are the fastest growing areas of the business?*

❏ *In this business, which career areas offer the fastest chance for promotion?*

When your network contact is interested enough to concentrate on your career needs, a different set of questions is appropriate.

The following questions are appropriate to use with a mentor, close associate or friend, or, in some happy instances, a new acquaintance who is willing to help a lot.

❏ *From what you know of my career up to now, what would be the logical next step?*

❏ *I have been thinking of (a specific position name) and wondered what your reaction would be.*

❏ *Do my qualifications contain any gaps that I should expand on?*

❏ *From what you know of me, is there anything that could give me a competitive advantage?*

❏ *Could you refer me to any other people who know about these positions?*

❏ The ultimate question, of course, is *"Do you know anyone who might be interested in seeing me?"*

If your questions have shown an inquiring attitude, it can seem natural to a friend, acquaintance or even a stranger.

Consider these networking tips

There are many common errors that people make while networking. Here are some points worth remembering.

❑ Getting through to people and making arrangements to see them isn't the victory. That comes only after you've completed a successful interview.

❑ Do your homework and be prepared. Know what you want to say and practice it first. Decide what strengths or achievements you want to get across.

❑ Be aware that most people today know when they're "being networked." That doesn't mean they won't help you. It only means you shouldn't try to fool them.

❑ Use your network right the first time around. Remember, they may also be needed in the future. Talk with people wherever you go—work, church, professional association meetings, casual get-togethers. Let people know that you are thinking about a new opportunity.

❑ Recognize that networking is part of the "job" of looking for a job. List the people you might want to get to see. Then, find a way to get someone to help you to them.

❑ Remember to keep your interviews brief. Ask for 10-minute appointments.

❑ If you are likely to forget your questions, try keeping them in a notebook.

❑ Try to leave every meeting with several more new names and, of course, always remember the names of secretaries.

❑ Send a handwritten thank-you note after your interview.

❑ Exchange business cards with those you meet. Keep a file of business cards. Follow every lead. Making advance judgment calls about a contact prior to a thorough investigation may short-circuit the networking process.

❑ Your primary network list should include your last employer's competition, because you are probably worth more to them than anyone else.

❑ Remember, networking is a proven way to search for a new job. Whenever you don't have other actions to take, you should be expanding your contacts.

Make sure you distinguish between networking among strangers and using your most important resource— your personal contacts.

"I was with a friend of mine today and I'm bringing him in to head up our new operations."

Here are some simple methods for getting help from others

Have you ever heard a job seeker say, "I've asked all of my friends to be on the lookout." *They honestly believe they've done everything they can to get help from them.*

If they thought about it though, they would realize that they have usually approached these friends on a very general basis and asked a favor which is next to impossible.

When they say, *"Let me know if you hear of anything, Joe."* Joe, of course, will keep his friend in mind, but probably only for a very short time. Five minutes later Joe is back to his routine, and his friend is forgotten.

However, the fact remains that Joe was probably willing and might have been able to help. How do you avoid the same mistake? Here are some simple principles that work. The first important thing you should do is select those who are likely to be your best supporters.

If you are a vice president, your best supporters are likely to be presidents of companies. If you're a controller, it is likely to be a VP of Finance. If you're just starting out, anyone with experience in your field of interest could prove helpful. Sometimes coincidence plays a role.

For example, an ambitious MBA in his late 20s took a job as a limousine driver three evenings a week. His assignments involved meeting executives at Newark Airport and driving them to their homes in New Jersey. By the eighth week of his part-time job, he had met 13 executives he could call.

Make your request sound important

Make your request sound important, but make sure your contact is a pleasant experience for others. People are far more likely to respond if you make it easy for them to assist you.

For example, you might ask a past associate if he knows of any managers among some growth companies you have identified. Or, you could ask a financial executive to review recent financial job openings with you and request permission to use his name in a cover letter.

On the other hand, you could ask a former customer to arrange letters of introduction to companies in his field. Then offer to draft a letter. Or, if you know someone in human resources, you could see if he would help by lending his name for contacting recruiters. Let them know how much your next position means to you, the jobs that interest you, the firms that appeal, and just what you want them to do.

Here is what one manager did. First, he wrote a brief note asking certain influential acquaintances to read his resume and make suggestions. Second, he requested a meeting and asked if it were possible for them to provide introductions to executives in firms they felt might be good targets.

Third, he asked each of them to send several letters to presidents of firms who were suppliers to their firms. He gave them a draft of a letter, and they gladly complied. By the way, if you are a senior executive and desire confidentiality, you might consider using an anonymous summary of your quali-fications, which would be sent out under the letterhead of a friend. This can work very well, especially if your friend has an impressive title.

How to get interviews through your references, and how to make the most of them.

Everyone I know is on the lookout for me!

Here's an example of how references can make the difference

Consider the story of Mark. His boss kept telling him he was worth more, but the firm was losing money. When Mark heard the company was to be sold, he felt his $45,000 salary was $15,000 less than it should be.

We helped make Mark aware of the power of his references. Would his boss be a good reference? And, did he feel bad about paying him less than he was worth? Absolutely! Could Mark ask him to act as his reference, and would he raise him to a level of $52,000 in return for his staying for the last two months? Yes, and that is what Mark asked for and got!

Now, the boss had a friend in an accounting firm. Mark asked his boss if he would approach his friend as a reference. Together, they visited over lunch. He was happy to act as a second reference for Mark. In the same way, Mark developed a third reference, his own brother-in-law.

When he launched a campaign, he had a good interview with the president of a small paper company. A conservative man, he asked for three references. Mark immediately recontacted his references, so they were ready. After his boss had given him a glowing reference, the president mentioned that he was still uncertain.

When the second reference was called *(the boss's friend)*, he told the president that in the right situation Mark could help save him a million dollars in taxes, as well as control costs.

He had repositioned Mark in the eyes of this president, from an accountant to a broader-based executive.

Next, Mark's third reference supported what the others said and added a few points. The day after the last reference check, he got a call from the president, and guess what? His message was, *"Mark, what will it take to get you?"* He ended up with a position as VP Finance at $60,000.

Identify your most important references

Most of the time, important references will be the people you reported to in the past, the person you currently report to or their superiors, and on rare occasions, the people who worked for you. Choose the highest level reference, as long as you get an enthusiastic endorsement, and avoid people who don't communicate well.

The references you select should know your background, be familiar with your achievements, and have no hesitation in making strong statements about you. Even though you may never have worked for them, respected people in a scientific discipline, directors of trade associations or magazine editors, all might be of help.

By the way, the ideal number of references to provide will depend strictly on your situation. In most cases, three references will suffice. At other times, the psychology you use may affect your decision. One person gave eight references to an executive and suggested that he select two or three to contact personally.

What your references may say is very important, but the enthusiasm and conviction they project when they say it is even more important!

Prepare your references with care

Be sure to let your references know that you have high regard for them and for their opinions. This will reinforce the positive chemistry between you and will make the references want to do their best for you.

Don't forget that even good references will know only part of your background. Make sure that they learn the full story. The importance of preparing your references carefully is well illustrated in the following example.

A young woman who had worked for me several years ago left to study for her MBA. She was competent and had a quiet manner, but could be forceful when needed. When she started interviewing, she was careful to bring me up to date on her activities. She also called to tell me that after an interview with a firm she liked, she felt they had some concerns about her quiet nature. Armed with that information, I was ready when I was called by the person who would be her boss.

Before the question was asked, I mentioned that sometimes people could be deceived by this woman's quiet nature, but that I had seen her assert herself time and again. The person, of course, responded positively, explaining that I had put to rest his one concern.

As a rule, you will submit the names of your references rather than presenting letters of recommendation. In the nonprofit, academic and government areas, however, it is traditional to collect written references. These endorsements are frequently required in politically sensitive situations.

Another point is that references are sometimes your best sources of referrals to employers. Leave them a half-dozen resumes. One thing you must do is reassure your references that you will not abuse the use of their names.

After calling your references, send a brief note that shows your appreciation and summarize a few positive things they can say about you. You can even prepare a list of questions that employers might ask your references and suggest answers for them. By the way, be sure to let references know as soon as you have used their name, and ask them to let you know when they have been contacted. This is important because employers will sometimes ask your reference for someone else who is familiar with your performance.

You need to be aware that reference checks are growing, and so are the use of credit reports. For positions paying less than $50,000, there is a 33% chance that a check will take place. Above $50,000, there is at least a 66% chance. At an executive level, search firms usually check references before submitting a candidate.

When checking, people may look to discuss your management style, ethics, work habits, people skills, liabilities, etc., in addition to confirming dates and incomes. Assume that employers will want to check your past superiors. Track these people down for at least the last three jobs or ten years. Don't be reluctant, even if you have not bothered to keep in touch. People like to learn what is happening to others.

In the case of executives who have moved into top management, references from any but the last one or two positions are rarely needed. Let the employer know that you need to keep your activity confidential. This lets them know you have a worthwhile position to protect.

If you have worked in only one job or for only one company for quite a long time, then contact former employees or bosses who have left your company and ask them to be references. If appropriate, consider using customers, suppliers or trade group contacts. In cases where you simply cannot offer references because of confidentiality, you can offer copies of positive performance appraisals.

Handling questionable references

It's long been said that bad references won't hurt as much as the good ones that turn out to be poor. If someone is apt to give you a bad reference, you need to bring it out in the interview and supply enough good ones to offset it.

For example, if the interviewer asks to speak with a reference who will be questionable, defuse the situation by explaining that you had differences of opinion on some managerial styles. Remain totally objective and unemotional, and never imply negatives about that person.

Also, if you are doubtful about what a reference might say, you might have a friend do a mock reference check to find out what is being said. If the reference is neutral, don't hesitate to ask the person to furnish more positive information.

If necessary, explain that their negative input is keeping you from winning a position and enabling you to support yourself and your family. As a last resort, you may have to imply that you will seek a legal remedy.

How to Get Employers to Create a Job That's Right for You

This is a great idea! We need someone to get this done— right now!

You can get offers, even if no job openings are said to exist. You simply need to present yourself as a solution to a problem.

An approach for those who want a job tailored to their best abilities

A few examples might include a technical person who can develop new products for a company, a sales executive with contacts in particular markets, or a general manager who can start up a division in a specific industry.

The "create a job" approach should also be considered by anyone who may have difficulty winning offers through other means. This includes those who have a narrow market for their talents; people who wish to change industries; those who have been unemployed for a while or who want to stay in a specific geographic or industry area.

In these situations, to win the job you want, you may have to create it by making an employer aware of your ability to make contributions.

You may fall into one or the other category, someone who "needs to" use this approach, or someone who simply "wants to" take advantage of its potential for them.

Regardless, keep in mind this simple thought. Employers hire people whenever they are persuaded that the benefit of having the person on board sufficiently outweighs the dollar cost. The following pages will give you some guiding principles as you consider this approach.

1 Focus on small to medium-sized firms

The first principle to understand is that to have your best chance at creating a job, your highest probability targets are likely to be small to medium-sized companies. This includes firms that are growing rapidly, bringing out new products, forming new divisions, acquiring other companies or reorganizing, etc.

These are the companies that need good people, often from other industries. They are free to make decisive moves quickly in response to opportunities. Large corporations are the least likely to respond to this approach. Budgets are usually allocated far in advance, and hiring practices tend to be relatively slow and methodical.

Of course, there are exceptions. All you need to do is assess your talents and contact the firms most likely to need you, regardless of their size or stability. And, if you know a market well or have talents in a particular function, just consider the industries where they would apply.

2 Reach the right high-level people

The second principle involves your reaching the appropriate high-level people. For example, you must be able to communicate directly with the person you would most likely work for, or their boss. In small and medium-sized companies, it would be someone at the vice president level or above. More often than not, the president would be involved.

I want you to talk to my V.P. about a new project I have in mind.

Entrepreneurs, of course, can create jobs. So can affluent individuals who often have large staffs and interests in many organizations. In a larger company, be sure to choose the person who has ultimate responsibility for the area in which you can contribute.

When selecting the person to contact, aim on the high side. If you're not sure who to contact, start with the president. When you make contact at this level, you must be ready to communicate a benefit proposition.

3 Get across your benefit proposition

The third principle is to make sure that you get across your benefit proposition. It must be an accurate, concise and easily understood description of what you can do for the company.

Your message has to hold the promise of tangible value on a scale large enough to warrant an investment in you. In that initial communication, you will also need to establish your credentials. Mention specific results you achieved in the past. They are the best indicators of what you can do in the future.

If you're a controller, you will obviously want to talk about how you can save money by cutting expenses. But, if you want someone to get interested enough to create a job for you, you'll stand a much better chance if you cite tangible results.

For example, your cost-cutting efforts led directly to a 5% increase in profits for your present employer; or that your studies showed the firm was losing a million dollars a year on three product lines they could easily drop.

When you hold out the promise for potential benefits of that size, it is obvious to the reader that you might well be worth the investment.

Likewise, if you've developed many successful products, that is all well and good. But, if you expect someone to create a job, you'll stand a much better chance if you can state that you spearheaded development of three products now representing 20% of sales, or that one now commands a 40% market share.

Achievements you cite don't have to be large, but they do have to be significant. For instance, if you are an office manager, you might state that you managed a smooth introduction of new systems that lifted staff productivity by 40%.

One of two keys to remember is that if you have an exciting idea to communicate, it may help if you can show how someone else has already used that idea successfully.

Dealing with opportunities is a key job for many executives. Most don't have enough time in the day, and they are predisposed to positive news from people who can help them. They will want to believe your message, so all you need do is make sure you provide positive reinforcement.

By the way, you can get your message across by phone or with a letter. Either way, make sure your "benefit position" is clear, easy to measure and significant; and be prepared to quickly establish your credentials.

4 Take strong initiatives in your first interview

Remember, your initial communication held out the promise of a significant benefit. What are your ideas? What makes you confident that they'll work? Do you really understand this company, its problems and opportunities?

Address these areas, but always remember to convey humility. Acknowledge that the other person has a better grasp of the problems facing the company than you could possibly have. This will help build positive rapport.

There are any number of simple phrases you might use. For example, you might say, *"I hope you didn't find my letter too presumptuous. No doubt, you've already given a lot of consideration to these areas."*

Or... "I took a calculated risk in telling you I could cut manufacturing costs. I recognize that every company is unique, and what works well in one may not work so easily in another."

Or... "I'm sure you've talked to many people who thought they knew your business better than you do. I don't mean to come across that way. I have a number of ideas, but let me first pay you the courtesy of listening to your opinion on these areas."

Comments like these set the stage for a cordial exchange of ideas. They can allow you to do the three things you need to accomplish in your first meeting.

They are as follows:

❏ Learn what the employer really wants.

❏ Build your rapport.

❏ Focus the employer's attention on the areas where you can help.

Your first goal is to find out how the employer views the problem. What does he see as the key challenges? What is the "hot button"? Where are the priorities as the employer sees them? What attempts have been made in the past? And, how much progress has already been made?

By asking a few questions and listening carefully, you will find out what the employer really wants. You will also be building rapport. Make sure you maintain a balanced conversation. Ask questions and make positive comments in response to the interviewer's remarks.

Most important, try to get the employer to share his innermost thoughts. Try to find out his vision for the organization. Only when he starts to think about this and the significant achievements he might realize, would he consider the possibility of creating a job.

If you are able to accomplish this in that first interview, that is enough. State that you would like to give things some further thought and clarify the benefits you bring to the situation. Show your enthusiasm, and get agreement that a second interview would be worthwhile. If you've done that, you're well on your way to having a job created for you.

Remember, in your second interview you must reinforce your value by drawing an unusually clear picture of the benefits you can bring. Then, you need to build enough enthusiasm to get an offer or be asked to speak with others.

5 Be sure to stir the employer's imagination

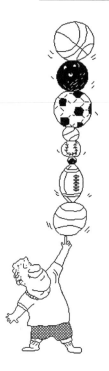

The fifth overall principle involves your need to stir the employer's imagination.

The employer should begin to anticipate specific benefits and be able to relate them directly to your talents. The entire focus of the conversation should be in the future, with the employer picturing a company already benefiting from your contributions.

Remember, the decision to create a job is as much emotional as it is intellectual. A dry recitation of proposed improvements won't be enough. You will have to convey enthusiasm and create a sense of excitement.

Of course, to do this you will have to refine your thinking, clearly identifying those areas the employer sees as most important. For each of them, be ready to discuss general approaches you would take to reinforce the notion that you will succeed. Your best way to do this is to tell stories about your past achievements.

If you build sufficient enthusiasm, the employer may conclude the meeting with a statement that he'd like to create a job for you. Or, he may ask you to meet with others in the company. If that happens, take the opportunity to build additional enthusiasm with every member of the team.

6 If you're not succeeding, try the "report option"

The sixth principle to keep in mind is that if you're not getting interest, try the "report option." Here, you need to make an offer to study the situation in more detail, perhaps to observe the company's operations or talk to knowledgeable outsiders, then to come back with a written report. The purpose? To make the entire subject more significant in the employer's mind.

It is the same principle used by management consultants, advertising agencies, top sales producers and others when they want to stimulate a company to action.

The very act of a study, and the presentation of a report following it, builds an aura of importance. Your report doesn't need to be lengthy, and it doesn't have to require a great deal of work.

It should, however, discuss the areas where you would hope to make significant contributions. For each of them, you would want to point out how you would proceed and the near-term benefits for the company. If you get interesting input from outsiders or cite examples which support your points, it will make your presentation more compelling.

If you try the report option, be sure to stage it properly. Let the employer think it's important, and ask for adequate time to present your findings. Your report, of course, would include a recommendation that a job be created. If the report is well received, you will have succeeded in creating a job.

In summary, you will never hit a home run unless you get into the game and go for it! The people in top management in most companies are well aware of the expenses involved in recruiting. When someone exceptional comes to their attention, many can and will act rapidly to create a job situation. This can involve the development of a new position or the shifting of someone of lesser competence in order to make room. Every day, with a little imagination, people are winning positions created under these circumstances.

How to Get Interviews by Telemarketing and Follow-up

Setting interviews over the phone is a lot easier than you think!

The phone is your key to getting the right interviews—fast!

Effective use of the phone is easier than you think. Of course, some people are totally confident in their ability to use the phone. However, 90% of all job seekers are reluctant to pick up the phone and make a "cold call."

If you're not experienced in using the phone, believe it or not, it's a mostly friendly and helpful world out there.

Most executives are courteous and polite and go out of their way to project a good image of themselves and their company. The same holds true for others such as secretaries or administrative assistants.

Still, there is a certain misconception that all secretaries and assistants will always keep you from speaking with their bosses. They do screen calls, but it is part of their job to make sure that contact is made when appropriate.

Throughout this chapter we'll refer to the term telemarketing. The difference between making simply phone calls and "telemarketing" is very basic. When you telemarket you have specific goals and you use a standardized procedure for making a large number of calls.

Proven telemarketing guidelines that work

Get used to making one call after another. Stand up and you'll give a power assist to your voice.

❑

You should do your phone work in batches, and you will need only one success each time to sustain your morale. To warm up, use some throw-away calls to get yourself started.

❑

Make sure you know how you will be answering your phone. List questions you may be asked and write out the answers to the difficult ones.

❑

You should also prepare a 30-second commercial of your most important selling points. Rehearse it. Tape it and critique it. Your effort will pay off.

❑

One of the best times to reach executives is very early in the morning or after 5:00 p.m. At that time, the switchboard is often still open, but many secretaries have departed; and the person you want may answer his or her own phone.

❑

Smile while speaking over the phone and your voice will sound more pleasant. Be friendly, enthusiastic and positive. When you encounter objections stay friendly, cooperative, and sometimes answer a question with a question.

Project a natural, confident tone—as you would when talking with a friend. Lower your voice. Speak slowly and don't give the impression you're rushed.

❏

Be prepared for rejection. Effective use of the phone is a numbers game. You can easily make 15 calls an hour.

❏

Be sure your phone is answered properly. No clever answering machine messages!

❏

The secretary doesn't really know who you are or your purpose. If you retain the thought that you only want advice and information, the decision maker has no reason to shy away from you. When speaking with the secretary, get her name and use it. Be confident, positive and polite.

❏

When following up, do not discuss your business other than to say the executive is expecting your call. Or use your job title to get by the secretary.

❏

If you begin to generate interest, do not reveal too much of your story. Remember, you want to press only for an interview, and never be interviewed on the phone.

Approaches for opening your conversations

The "good news" approach

 Mr. Ellis: When I heard about your four quarters of record growth...

Here you build a positive relationship based on specific "good news." Everyone likes to have good things happen and to hear from others who are enthusiastic about their good fortune. You can be sure that your message will immediately help to build a feeling of friendliness and warmth over the phone. This kind of approach can play an important role in winning extra interviews and getting people to help you.

The "third-party" approach

 Mr. Ellis: Bill Regan, a partner with Arthur Andersen, thought I should get in touch with you.

If you mention the name of a third party who knows the person you're calling, it helps to establish rapport, but it's also helpful even when they don't know each other. The approach is simple. It might go like this: *"Bill Regan, a partner with Arthur Andersen, thought I should get in touch with you. He felt your growth not only suggests a good investment but might indicate a good employment possibility. His insights prompted me to follow up with you personally. Do you have a moment?"*

The "specific reason" approach

 Mr. Ellis, I have a specific reason for calling you.

Anyone who has experience in getting things done can consider using this "specific reason" approach. It's straightforward and can go like this: *"Mr. Franklin, I have a 'specific reason' for calling you. I know the line of business you are in and something of the processes you use. During the past 15 months, I have been able to save a company like yours approximately $850,000. I would like to share the details with you. Does your calendar permit a meeting later this week?"*

"Perhaps you can help me"

Hi, Mr. Ellis, I'm Tom Cole. Perhaps you can help me. Since the position has already been filled, could you refer me to...

If a specific opening has already been filled, someone can help you meet a hiring official in another part of the company. If the individual you contact does not have a precise fit in his department, perhaps he could help you meet a person in another division. If you are told that the person you want to speak to is out, the best response is, *"Thanks. Perhaps you can help me. When is a good time to call back?"*

Tips for handling people who screen your call

 ☎ As previously mentioned, start by using the name of the person who is the "screener." Once a person knows he or she has been identified, their manner will become more personal.

☎ When asked your name, identify yourself with an organization if possible.

☎ Remember, the more difficult and expert the screener is, the more valuable that person is likely to be, especially as an ally in your future relationships with the firm.

☎ If you don't get through on your first attempt, and you can't get a suitable time to call back, suggest a time when you will call the screener back. In all cases, until you have established direct contact, don't leave messages.

☎ When you call back, use the screener's name with the receptionist. After establishing that the person is difficult to reach, try this procedure: *"Since he (or she) is so hard to reach, would you do me a small favor? May I call back at _____ to see if he would be interested in speaking with me for a few minutes?"* If you must leave a message, leave one of potential benefit to the person you are calling.

☎ Consider reversing your attempt to speak with the decision-maker by asking for an internal referral to another line manager in the area in which you might want to work for the company.

☎ If the screener refers you to personnel, get the name of the person to whom you will be speaking. Call back later for that person or request an immediate transfer.

☎ After a few minutes of discussion, ask two or three penetrating questions about the company's needs. When asked difficult questions, those who don't know the answer are more inclined to refer you to an appropriate line manager.

☎ After a few days, you can also call back the screener and explain that while the personnel people were helpful, they were not really able to answer the questions you had in mind.

☎ You may encounter the question: "Are you looking for a job?" The answer might be: *"Yes, I am; do you think you could help me? Though I'm employed, a friend suggested your firm to me."*

☎ Or, you may encounter the comment, "We don't have any openings at the present time." The response: *"I appreciate a person who is direct; however, I have such a strong interest in the firm, I really believe that with your recent growth, I could be a great asset. Will you allow me to tell you why?"*

Some openers for use after you reach the right person

"We'd like to honor you for being the only job hunter to get through every barrier ... and reach our boss!"

❑ Considering what is happening to the technology of our business, I know I can be very useful to you because of my training and experience in _____.

❑ From your Annual Report, I read that the company's expanding in the _____ area. That's an area where I could help, and I wanted to schedule an appointment.

❑ My friend _____ suggested that I make a point of contacting you. You may recall from my letter that I have experience in _____ that might be of help to you.

❑ With my background in _____ and the recent news about _____, I thought I should try to get in touch with you. Could you suggest a convenient time? Do you have 20 minutes before you get started some morning next week?

❑ Mr. _____, your company has a tremendous reputation for market-leading products. I'd like very much to visit with you to explain how I could contribute to that reputation through my work in _____. Do you have a half hour free this Tuesday?

How you can turn rejection letters into interviews

Less than 1% of all job hunters ever follow up a rejection letter. This gives you a big opportunity. Follow-up requires a special tenacity, a certain "thickness of skin," and an ability to accept rejection as a challenge. The person who has arrived at the perfect company should be prepared to do the following.

Find out all about the firm from every source available; call, write, visit, speak to as many people as necessary; go through third-party channels; and depart from conventional approaches. Here are three approaches that might fit your personality or circumstance.

"Acting puzzled & helpless"

This does not call for much acting ability for many of us, because it is the way we feel when we receive those politely worded notes that give us the bad news that our services are not required. We are puzzled because we cannot understand how they can't recognize our qualities, and we are helpless to do much about it.

One way to follow up is to call and thank the sender of the letter for their reply. Then try to engage them in a frank discussion as to your failure to understand what is going on. The usual explanation is that there are no vacancies available at the present time.

However, you must not let this reply end the conversation. You must try to keep it going. What almost everyone in a job search needs is a preliminary, non-obligatory talk with a person who is qualified to explain what the company does and how it goes about meeting its employment needs.

This is what you should ask for, because as a puzzled and helpless person, you do not know what to do next! Here is how this might work.

Mr. Jones, I got your letter this morning and it tells me that you are going to keep my resume on file against further openings. I'm a bit puzzled at that because I only sent a short note to the company suggesting a meeting to talk about what I might be able to do for you.

This must be delivered without a trace of sarcasm because that could kill your relationship. Then, keep quiet and see what the answer may be. Silence is powerful. Carrying on from here, find out how the organization goes about recruiting. People enjoy giving advice, especially when sincerely asked by someone who really needs it.

For example, you might ask *...does the company ever employ people with my disciplines and experience? Do they advertise jobs, or do they place people in the company from other sources? If so, which recruiters do they use?*

These questions are asked because you do not know the answers, not because you are trying to be "smart." There is still enough warm feeling in even the most harassed executive hearts for you to get some very useful information from them.

What you are seeking is specific information, such as the names of heads of departments; plans for expansion; ideas for approaching personalities; the real "stuff" that the company is made of. With that information you can then approach someone else or keep it on file for follow up next month.

"I need your understanding"

This approach is very straightforward and involves asking some simple direct questions.

Was it correct to send my letter to the president in the first place? Does the Personnel Department really handle recruitment at my level and in my discipline? It is important for me to know this, because I may well have approached the company incorrectly.

How should I go about reaching the right decision maker?

A young person should request information or assistance in reaching the right person by talking with lower levels of management. Executives should get into the upper levels by asking who handles specific responsibilities.

Here's another example:

Mary, I really need your help and I can sense that you would like to help me if you could. But what I must find out is this: how do I get to talk to Harry Smith for a few minutes at a time when he can listen to me or arrange to meet me?

Charm is the watchword— patience in building relationships, careful listening and projecting a positive attitude which will create a warm response.

"Acting very assertive"

Mary, I was surprised to learn this morning that you had sent my letter addressed to Mr. Jones to your Personnel Department! What happened? My note simply suggested a meeting with Mr. Jones. By now it may be all over the company that I am looking for a job!

This could sound too strong if not said with a smile! If you don't get the response you need go on. For example...

What we ought to do is this: I need your help to recover the letter from Personnel and have Mr. Jones look at it himself. Obviously, he is the man I must see. Can we do something about that?

Should I write to him again and mention what has happened? Perhaps I could send you a copy with a note to give it to him?

Another way of using this style is to say...

I must speak to Mr. Jones right away, Mary. This is serious. Someone has sent a confidential letter that I addressed to him to other people in your organization and that worries me very much. This frequently makes the breakthrough, so be ready with your telephone script for him or her.

A sample script for trying to reach the right person

Okay, so now you have called and been put through to the secretary. Off we go...

Hello Ms. Jones, is Bill in? I'm _____. He should be expecting my call.

May I ask what this is in reference to?

I wrote to him last week, and in my letter I promised to call him today. It concerns an urgent matter for me.

If you are looking for a job, it would have been sent to the Human Resources Department.

Mary, if I need to talk to H.R., who can really put me in the picture there? I need the Director, I guess.

She tells you what you want to know and puts you through. It's Jim _____.

Jim, I'm _____. I've just been talking to Bill Smith's office, and Mary told me I should be talking to you. I'd written Bill and suggested a meeting, but he's apparently sent my note to you.

What can I do for you?

I wanted to meet with Bill because I believed that he would be the right person to talk to. There are several reasons for this; they have to do with what I can do for _____ Co.

Be prepared to tell Jim enough to put him in the picture.

Of course, I could be wrong in seeking to talk with Mr. _____ himself. You know more about the company than I do. Jim, I need your help. How does the company go about bringing in new people at my level? In my current job, I am responsible for _____ .

Consider this response from Jim:

I'm sorry. We don't need anyone at the levels you've mentioned. In any case, all promotion here is from within the company. We don't have anything here right now... sorry.

Now you can keep a discussion going as follows:

Jim, I was afraid you'd tell me that, but you know, there are plenty of cases where companies do bring in outside people at senior levels. How do I find out what to do to take this further? Isn't there some way to get an exploratory talk at *an appropriate level? I need your help.* (Or if you can't get anywhere... *if you can't help me somehow, could you give me Bill Smith's office again. I need to speak to him again.*)

Then... *Hi Mary! I'm afraid Jim can't help me. Basically, what I'm looking for is one piece of information—one person to address, someone who will take a few moments to talk to me, someone who will explain your system there. Is there someone else I should approach first before addressing Bill?*

She may transfer you to someone else at this point. Now consider what to do if she says:

He asked me to tell you that he would like to see your resume. *My resume? Well, that was not what I had in mind, Mary. However, is there a chance I could have a brief word with him now? It's really important.*

If this doesn't work, send a note and confirm that you will call. Then, renew your contact with the secretary.

She may say... oh yes, he asked me to tell you that he is unable to meet you but he appreciates your interest.

I see. Mary, I really have a problem. It could be that Bill is not the person I should have addressed in the first place. Is there anyone else I should be speaking to? For example, who is the head of the _____ Department?

(What you are looking for is another source of information. Of course, Mary might say He asked me to tell you that he's having Personnel circulate your resume. This is plausible, but watch out.)

Mary, I have some misgivings about that. I'm concerned about confidentiality. Frankly, I expected to speak with him before we went further. Is he there right now? (You are pressing, but politely. If you are an executive, you could adopt the attitude of concern about loss of privacy.)

Mary... If you circulated my letter that means others in the firm are going to know that I'm even contacting you. I'd better speak to Mr. _____ right now!

Of course, if you are put through, you will drop your concerned attitude and simply explain why you needed to keep the entire matter confidential.

In your calls you need to mean business. Always be very pleasant and polite but quite prepared to take further action. These are not casual calls. Never be deterred by lower staffers or "standard practices." Be willing to ask for assistance, but ask for it in specific terms, expecting answers and cooperation. Stay with these principles. They work!

In summary, being able to work the phone effectively is an essential part of a professional job search. As we have pointed out, you need to use the phone as a way for setting interviews, networking, making your direct mail work and for following up. Make it a point to become a pro on the phone. Your confidence will soar and your job search will suddenly turn up exciting new possibilities.

How to Develop Your Personal Action Plan for Getting Interviews

At the heart of the professional job search is your need for an action plan. It will enable you to job hunt with far less strain, confusion or worry.

Introduction— The concept behind an action plan is simple

The very idea of a personal action plan was practically unknown a decade ago. Today, however, it makes a lot of sense for anyone entering the job market. Having a personal action plan allows you to take job hunting actions systematically to produce better results.

The concept behind a personal action plan is simple. There are no gimmicks involved and it doesn't require forecasting the future. Rather, it is a process for planning job hunting actions, then following through in a way that will bring you a greater number of interviews.

For the purposes of this discussion, we'll assume that you will soon settle on your career and industry directions and your financial goals. At this point, therefore, we want to focus on how you should plan actions that will develop interviews.

A personal action plan should have both a goal and a timetable. For most people the goal is getting a better job.

The time can vary, depending upon the amount of research you need to do; but for most people it usually involves an effort to get from Point A, where you are not, to Point B, which is an offer of a new job in 6 to 13 weeks.

Of course, a longer time period may be preferred by some who may need time to gradually refine their goals or who are searching at six-figure levels.

Think about job hunting in a new way

Without an action plan, chances are you will spend too much energy on a series of haphazard actions, trusting to fate that you'll get the results you want. Planning, on the other hand, brings focus to your efforts and allows you to control your actions and your destiny in the job market.

Consider for a moment how products and services are successfully sold to corporations. In most cases a marketing plan is followed. In your job search you are also selling. In this case the service is your combination of talents, experience and knowledge, and the potential buyers are various organizations.

On the next page you'll see a simple outline of the parallels between your situation and the marketing of a "big ticket service" by a large firm.

With this process in mind, to help assure your success, it is wise to shoot for 15 or more interview opportunities. When you have this many things to look into, it puts you in control. The best way to make sure this happens is to execute a carefully thought out action plan.

If you want to choose between 3 or 4 offers, as a rule you'll need to gear your action plan to generate 15 to 20 interview opportunities.

Five key elements are critical in any marketing effort

You are the product. You must surface all product information. You've got to dig deep to understand each aspect of what you have to offer in the marketplace and how to handle every liability.

Our success involved our product, its positioning, our promotions, our pricing and our distribution.

You must position yourself. This expression refers to who your products and services are targeted for. It means you have to know which potential buyers you are going to appeal to. You very seldom see a successful product that claims it can do anything for anyone. So, position your talents toward meeting specific needs of employers.

Your need to promote yourself. After you have a good understanding of where you want to go and why, some promotional material is required. Decide what you want to communicate, and get your resumes and letters created.

You need to price yourself. Keep in mind that while your income potential will ultimately be determined by supply and demand, you can dramatically enhance your value through effective promotion and negotiation.

You need to place your credentials. This is a distribution concept. In other words, how will you get your message out, and where will it go? Will you go directly to employers or through middlemen? There are many avenues of distribution you can use, with options in each of them.

Your main action avenues for reaching employers

There are many ways for generating interviews with employers. A very small percentage of the market can be reached through school placement services, through placing ads for yourself, through computer job listing or matching services and the like. This discussion is about the primary steps you can take for putting your credentials into the marketplace— the actions that can yield a significant quantity of the right interviews. They include:

Direct mail marketing to employers— "macro" approach
Direct mail marketing to employers— "micro" approach

Employers to initially contact by telemarketing

Mailings to recruiters

Ads to answer— from previous 13 weeks & ongoing

Employers to contact from spot opportunities

Networking— friends / acquaintances
Networking— by industry and influentials

Planning for direct mail marketing

For your initial macro or large mailing, plan for a minimum of 100 total contacts for each $10,000 of income you're seeking. It may be wise to double that number if you are in the higher income ranges or if you're attempting a major career change.

About four weeks after your large mailing, your next step will involve sending highly customized letters directed toward a smaller number of companies who are at the top of your priority list. Depending on the size of your list, this effort might be restricted to your best of the best. Typically, here you are talking about 15 to 20% of your entire list of targeted prospects.

Contacting recruiters

Your mailings to employers should be well under way before you start initiating action with recruiters. For those with marketable backgrounds who are conducting a regional campaign, substantial contacts with recruiters are normally recommended. The rule to follow here is to plan to contact as many as your time and budget permits.

Keep in mind that recruiters will not be of much help to people looking to change careers. They can be very effective for people with good track records who seek to make moves that are compatible with their previous career and industry experience. Once again, it is essential that you review Chapter Four on recruiters before proceeding.

Answering ads

Once your initial mailings to employers and recruiters is underway, you should answer newspaper ads that have appeared over the last 13 weeks. Your level of activity here will depend upon the type of position you are seeking and the number of geographic areas you want to cover.

As you go through your search, answering ads should be worth no more than 10% of your effort, but it should be treated as importantly as the other action areas. While answering ads can be an effective avenue for some, it will yield nothing for others. Be sure to review Chapter Three and our strategies for answering ads.

Responding to spot opportunities

As previously discussed, most positions are filled before they ever get advertised or turned over to recruiters. Our separate review of unadvertised jobs should give you all the direction you need to uncover spot opportunities.

Needless to say, as you identify these situations, the names of these organizations should be added to your priority list of employers. As a rule, your plan should include time for identifying and responding to as many of these situations as possible.

Networking

You should not plan on networking until you have gotten your search well underway. In the course of doing that, you may refine your goals or materials.

Chapter Seven on networking will provide you with everything you need about how to network among your contacts and acquaintances. If you are employed and want to use this action avenue, you should plan on initiating six to ten contacts by telephone each week. If you are organized, you will need very little time to accomplish this.

If you are not working you can do much more. Remember, the best networking efforts are very focused and usually have target industries in mind. Contacting influential people should also be part of most job campaigns.

Taking stock of your progress

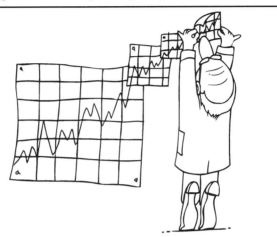

As you go through your job search, you need to continually take stock of your progress. Are you keeping up with the plan? Are you getting positive feedback on your materials? Have you gotten reinforcement that the goals you've set are indeed realistic?

Make notes and then determine whether it might be time for some fine tuning or adjustments. If so, make them.

If you haven't already accepted a new job after six to eight weeks, weigh all of your activity and results. At that time, you should either commit to another six to eight weeks following the same approach or modify your plan based on what you've found out.

Depending on your circumstances, you may be close to an offer, or you may not have made much progress, in which case you'll need to reaffirm commitment to a campaign philosophy with a "whatever it takes" attitude. As long as your goal remains unchanged and you remain committed to reaching it, determination is the key that will ultimately get you there.

Creating your own action plan

Here is an easy-to-use planner that can help you design your campaign efforts, as well as measure your activity on a week-by-week basis.

The best way to approach this plan is to decide first on the priority you wish to give your job campaign. If you are out of work, severely underemployed or about to relocate, then it should receive top priority. If this is your situation, design an aggressive campaign—one that can potentially produce more activity than you really need. Start with a six-week time schedule.

On the other hand, if you are currently employed and working 60 hours a week, you may wish to design a campaign plan over a 12-week period. In this instance the amount of action you take will be dictated by the time you expect to have available for interviewing.

Job hunting is a numbers game. The more good contacts you make, the more good opportunities you will have to explore. Those who arrive at the right time, whose personalities mix, and who appear the best qualified are the ones who get the jobs.

Enter your projected total number of contacts in the "Total Planned" column. Break down this total into what you plan to do each week. Be realistic. At the end of each week, see if you are on track. If not, then modify your plan.

Personal action plan for the first six weeks

Primary activity channels	Total Planned	Actions by week					
		1	2	3	4	5	6
1 Direct mail—your mass approach							
2 Select phone follow-up on the above							
3 Advertisements to answer							
4 Your mailing to recruiters							
5 Contacts from spot opportunities							
6 Networking—friends / acquaintances							
7 Networking—by industry & influentials							
8 Custom direct mail w / follow up							

Recap of results

Primary activity channels	Total Replies	Positive Replies	Interviews	Offers
1 Direct mail—your mass approach				
2 Select phone follow-up on the above				
3 Advertisements to answer				
4 Your mailing to recruiters				
5 Contacts from spot opportunities				
6 Networking—friends / acquaintances				
7 Networking—by industry & influentials				
8 Custom direct mail w / follow up				

Job hunting is a numbers game. The more contacts you make— the more situations that come your way. An action plan helps keep you on track. Here are a few case histories.

At $54,000—
A market research director

Victoria had been employed since college by a consumer products firm. Her campaign took 10 weeks, and it involved selective use of all marketing channels. Because there were only a few consumer product manufacturers in her area, she decided to look into opportunities with service companies. She devoted part of every day to her campaign. Her efforts were well targeted and resulted in a total of 42 positive inquiries and 18 opportunities for interviews. She received five job offers.

Her best offer came through a networking contact with a celebrity in L.A. who referred her to an excellent situation. She made little advance use of her resume because of her one-industry experience. However, her use of letters and careful targeting of firms worked perfectly. The resume she presented at interviews was based on the example on page 174.

Action Channel	Contacts Initiated	Positive Response
1 Employers contacted by direct mail		
(A) Mass approach	250	7
(B) Custom approach	25	5
2 Employers contacted by telemarketing	50	4
3 Recruiters contacted	55	7
4 Ads answered	18	2
5 Employers contacted by response to spot opportunities	25	11
6 Networking contacts initiated		
(A) Friends/Acquaintances	20	3
(B) Influentials/Industry	15	3

At $175,000–
A senior executive

Franklin was an unemployed financial executive in search of a six-figure income. He launched a large direct mail campaign to both recruiters and employers. He made use of various cover letters with two resumes that were identical to the style on pages 174 and 198. His mailing went out during the first weeks of his campaign. He then followed up his best prospects by phone.

While waiting for responses, he made a strong effort at contacting acquaintances and seeking referrals. He handled this by mail and then used telephone follow-up. With spot opportunities, he started with phone contact, forwarded a letter with a resume and then followed up again. His campaign produced a total of 53 positive inquiries. Over 11 weeks, he interviewed for 13 situations. Those resulted in three job offers and compensation at a 30% higher level.

Action Channel	Contacts Initiated	Positive Response
1 Employers contacted by direct mail		
(A) Mass approach	3700	17
(B) Custom approach	150	4
2 Employers contacted by telemarketing	25	6
3 Recruiters contacted	350	5
4 Ads answered	20	1
5 Employers contacted by response to spot opportunities	25	5
6 Networking contacts initiated		
(A) Friends/Acquaintances	40	10
(B) Influentials/Industry	30	5

At $28,000–
A teacher changing careers

Carolyn ran a campaign based on spot opportunities and direct mail and focused on Manhattan. She used two different resumes (a two-page functional resume based on the example on page 196 and a one-page resume similar to the example on page 181). Handwritten memos were attached.

Her resumes and phone work were the key to her success. She had an excellent story about her communication skills and the fact that she was a quick study and very good on her feet. During her campaign Carolyn built a network of valuable contacts. It took her eight weeks to find the right job. Four offers were developed, and she became manager of the largest temporary office facility in the city. The job involved inside sales and management of the administrative staff. It also brought her daily contact with many interesting personalities.

Action Channel	Contacts Initiated	Positive Response
1 Employers contacted by direct mail		
(A) Mass approach	385	14
(B) Custom approach	0	0
2 Employers contacted by telemarketing	0	0
3 Recruiters contacted	0	0
4 Ads answered–local	4	0
5 Employers contacted by response to spot opportunities	80	21
6 Networking contacts initiated		
(A) Friends/Acquaintances	10	3
(B) Influentials/Industry	0	0

Section Three: Resumes and Letters

The next section is about your creative work— your resumes and letters. They are the fuel that makes everything go according to plan. Make no mistake about it, in today's marketplace they need to be as good as you can possibly make them.

Princeton/Masters has a unique and highly effective approach to resumes and letters. However, before you start writing, review Chapter Two. It will help make sure you capture everything that's marketable about you.

Creating Outstanding Resumes and Letters: A New and More Effective Way

Why a few people can succeed with very average resumes

I used to always marvel about how bad some people's resumes were, yet how well they did in the job market. Then one day I first discovered that your need for a superior resume operated in reverse order to the following criteria.

First, are those who have achieved what I call celebrity status. These are basically people whose reputations precede them in whatever world of work in which they exist.

Second, are those who are either well enough known, or who have such extensive contacts, that they can land jobs directly through their contacts. After all, when someone really knows you, they may not need a resume, or if they do, any summary you can put out in a hurry will meet their needs.

Third, are those who have what I call an industry hook or high-demand specialty. Needless to say, if you're an expert on my business, and I can use some help, then let's talk.

Fourth, are the top producers in any field, the people who can simply call and say, "this is what I've done for others... I'm a pro... I can do the same or better for you."

Now, if you fit in one of the above categories, you can skip this chapter. However, if you are in the other 97% — then the information that follows is very important for you.

Most people cannot succeed with old approaches to resumes

It used to be that any professional, manager or executive could sit down at a typewriter and knock out an acceptable resume in a few hours. You could then answer some ads, send them to some agencies and recruiters, and distribute them to friends and family.

You might even send some off to America's bigger companies who were growing in every industry and had job openings faster than they could fill them.

However, the 60s, 70s and 80s are over, and the job market will never be the same again.

The cumulative effects of international competition, the decline of the dollar and the shift to a service economy have changed the rules. Middle management jobs are being eliminated as company after company goes through reorganizations and tries to become lean and mean.

But that's only part of the story. The number of people seeking professional-level jobs keeps growing. Each year 500,000 or so college graduates come into the market. In addition, the percentage of married women who work continues to expand.

What's more, with the explosion in the number of personal computers *(which only got a big push when the first IBM PC was introduced in 1982),* many people now distribute resumes in very big numbers.

What does all of this mean for you? Well, the number of resumes circulated relative to the number of attractive professional, managerial and executive jobs available is going up and up, and will continue to go up and up.

165

As mentioned earlier, hundreds of people are apt to answer every good ad. As many as 40,000 resumes arrive each month at offices of some of the major executive search firms. In short, the competition is intense. The fact is, that even with an excellent economy, the competition will continue to increase throughout the rest of the '90s.

Now, when you look for a job, unfortunately, you are reduced to how you look on paper.

Fortunately for you, over 95% of all resumes are far less effective than they should be. They are average in appearance, disclose far too many liabilities, and are rarely interesting or imaginative. Worst of all, a single resume is usually expected to work with all types of audiences, and it doesn't!

And fortunately for you again, this discussion will give you just what you need to have a major advantage in the resume area— at least until every one gets up to date like you will be. But that's not about to happen for at least another ten years or more.

The nature of this resume system — why narratives are the best style

There is so much advice available on resumes that the annual words on this subject must qualify for the Guiness Book of Records. Just think of the millions of spouses and friends who are asked each year if someone's resume looks good and who happily give their opinion and advice!

Nevertheless, my previous experience as an advertising copywriter and my consulting experience in working with thousands of people, measuring what really excels, what does all right, and what does poorly, has led me to a rather important philosophy.

You see, I believe in narrative resumes that are written in a style that is similar to a letter and that are almost always two pages. The length depends on the situation and how narrow or broad a person's market really is. What's more, if a one-page resume is required, it must carry the same story, with no abbreviation from the basic and best story that can be written.

The first reason I prefer a narrative is because it seems like less of a sales pitch than resumes which are full of dashes, bullets, abrupt statements, too much bold type, etc. I know how much my clients want good jobs, but one of the keys to getting them is to never seem too available or a candidate for just anything. *Who wants to hire someone who isn't wanted by a lot of others?*

The resumes that work best are ones that make you sound articulate, that never simply scream a bunch of facts and which tell a story, preferably a persuasive one.

The second reason I like a narrative is that it seems more personal, more dignified and more professional. Needless to say, the closer it comes to a letter, the more personal and readable your resume will seem.

The third reason I like it is that it enables me to more easily avoid disclosing any liabilities my clients may have *(things which might rule them out, and they'll never know why!).*

The fourth reason I prefer a narrative is that it truly is the only format which I can call a "solution resume." Using this style, I can craft the best story in support of the objective my client has. What's more, if we decide on an alternate objective, such as a general manager instead of a VP sales, then it is relatively easy to slant it into a second document .

The same holds true for preparing all the types of letters you might need in a job search. Once you have written your narrative resume, you can adapt the same words and phrases for your letters.

The fifth and last reason a narrative is the Vitamin C for job hunters is that it simply works best in the four major environments that you are likely to encounter. They include these situations:

❑ When your resume is used as a leave-behind— after you've finished an interview, and when it is likely to be circulated to others along with the impressions of the first party.

❑ When it is provided after you met an employer— at the beginning of, or during an interview.

❑ When it is provided for personal contacts to endorse and distribute.

❑ And, when it is sent out cold to employers or recruiters— the areas where it has to really perform.

If you give a moment to thinking about these situations, and you look at all the other styles you might use, you'll quickly see why a narrative is really the best solution— and truly the resume for all seasons.

Here's what you need to do

Start off by accepting the fact that your resume needs to be great! This discussion will give you all you need to make it that way. Then accept the fact that you are going to need a number of resumes to get the most out of your marketability.

Here are the resumes you need in support of each objective in today's competitive marketplace.

First, you should have a very strong two-page narrative resume— one that can be used for your very best prospects in traditional industries and organizations.

Second, if you want to be a candidate for jobs in creative industries such as ad agencies, design firms, publishers, broadcasting, film studios, television, etc., then you'll need a narrative resume with more of a creative flair. After all, creative ability is more highly valued in those firms.

Third, if you want to do extensive networking, you should really take advantage of a special-looking narrative resume that will work best for this specialized purpose.

Fourth, for lower and mid-level professionals, if you intend to contact firms who receive volumes of resumes (*like employment agencies, recruiters or trade associations*) then you will also need a one-page narrative resume.

Last, but not least, accept the fact that for a second career option you may wish to explore, you'll need the same set of resumes to qualify you for that particular goal.

Now, here is the good news. These resumes can have the very same words. They simply need to have different visual "looks" to maximize their response among different audiences.

Illustrating this new resume system

One resume won't work best for every purpose. So, having several resumes will give you a major advantage!

First write one two-page narrative resume for the traditional employers you might consider. Then don't change a word, but create visually different resumes— similar to the examples on the next pages.

They present one person's original resume, and then show you the new resumes developed under this system.

Old resume— a "before" example

This was the original resume before converting to our system. Far better than most resumes, it had a clear objective, along with a short summary of her main qualifications. It was backed up with functional information relating to her goal.

J. Katherine Gibbs
7777 E. Evans Avenue, Apt. #I 201
Denver, CO 80231
(303)   671-8200

Objective: Assistant to Senior Executive

30 years old, B.A. Denison University
Complete office management, secretarial professional executive, computer skills, experience in accounting, advertising communications and planning of special events and conferences.

Personal qualities include very diversified capabilities; effective with staff at all levels including Board members. Exceptional integrity and polarity.

Assisting Senior   Executives

- Prepared personal financial statements;
- Managed personal finances and was authorized to make transfer on all bank accounts.
- Handled IRS audits, preparation of taxes for accountants, prepared financial affidavit for attorneys.
- Supervised secretarial staff on a variety of special projects. Reviewed resumes and interviewed candidates for secretarial positions.

Accounting

- Accounts Payable: reconciled accounts; researched payment problems.
- Calculation of sales commissions.
- Preparation of payroll and assisted the Controller on special projects.

Special   Events/ Conferences

- Planned or assisted with of the following events: Cypress Golf Course Japanese Groundbreaking Ceremony, Coors Classic, VailAmerica Days, WinterFaire and VailRocks.
- Responsible for scheduling and planning in state/out of state client conferences nationwide for the president, including coordinating meeting dates and location with the clients, securing meeting space, working with hotel

---

However, her resume was a series of bullets and did not tell a strong story. For example, on page one she listed accounts payable experience. Compare it to the explanation at the top of page two on her new resume.

J. Katherine Gibbs...page 2

sales and catering managers, preparing presentation materials, and making travel arrangements.

General Office Management

- Coordinated with various outside database services. Ordered information and distributed it to national and regional facilities.

- Served as project manager for development of an extensive national database and subsequently oversaw computer operations and distribution of information to the field. Worked with all levels of sales and field personnel to solve problems.

- Supervised a fast paced front office. Responsibilities included: hiring temporary staff, booking appointments for sales staff, meeting and greeting clients, telemarketing to out-of-state potential clients and dispatching 100-200 incoming calls on 15 phone lines for three organizations.

Public Relations/ Advertising

- Managed all media placement for an in-house advertising agency.

- Coordinated ad placements with major print media throughout the U.S., negotiated print advertising contracts for the firm, coordinated production of mechanicals with creative staff, placed on average, 30 advertisements on a weekly basis.

- Handled all billing verifications. Also had fiduciary responsibility for issuing payments for approximately $400,000 annually.

- Participated in numerous seminars and workshops in the area of advertising and public relations.

Employment History

Arnold Palmer Enterprises	1990 to Present
Bennington, International	1988-1990
Vail Resort Association	1985-1988
Ketchum Public Relations	1983-1985

Personal

Single, in excellent health and physical condition. Enjoy a variety of leisure activities. These include: mountain biking, skiing, theater, world travel and current events.

New "all purpose" narrative resume

This was her primary resume. With a clean professional appearance, it reads more like a letter and tells a thorough, interesting and convincing story. Once completed, the rest of the resumes have the same words with different "looks."

J. Katherine Gibbs
7777 E. Evans Avenue, Apt. I 201
Denver, Colorado 80231
(303) 671-8200

> Optional
> postage
> stamp size
> photo

Assistant to Senior Executive / Executive Secretary / Office Management

Experienced professional at working for senior executives. Complete office management and secretarial skills. My work experience includes work in accounting, advertising, communications, public relations and planning of special events and conferences. Competence with dictating equipment, IBM and Macintosh systems, Word Perfect, Microsoft Word, Microsoft Excel and Great Plains Accounting Software.

Personal qualities include a high level of integrity, dependability, loyalty and trust in matters of confidence. Highly organized and service-oriented, I have been effective with staff at all levels from entry level professionals to Board Members. Excellent phone presence. Capable of working under tight deadlines and meeting high performance goals. Cultured, polished and well-traveled.

My Experience in Assisting Presidents, COOs and CEOs

I have worked directly for the Presidents of two service businesses; a publishing and consulting firm who licensed a dozen offices throughout the U.S. and an international golf course design firm. In both situations my role involved a wide range of assignments—all related to enhancing the President's productivity and achievement of his personal and corporate goals. Some of my responsibilities have included:

■ Prepared personal financial statements and expense reports; managed personal finances including authority to make substantial transfers involving personal bank accounts; assisted in IRS audits; prepared tax information for accountants and financial affidavits and reports for attorneys. Coordinated stock purchases and brokerage matters with Merrill Lynch, Bear Stearns and Goldman Sachs.

■ Routinely acted as a Project Manager overseeing secretarial staffs who were assigned a variety of projects of special interest to the President. Also assisted with recruiting and screening of administrative professionals, and ran the President's appointment schedule and screened all calls.

■ Regularly interfaced with all levels of internal corporate staff on behalf of the company Presidents, and also with major clients, the company's legal advisors, major vendors and auditors, including Arthur Anderson and Ernst & Young.

■ Have personally represented and traveled for Presidents on matters of confidence, public relations and administrative assignments. This includes work in Denver, New York, London and the West Coast. It has also involved major foreign clients from Japan as well as English speaking countries.

Most people need something similar to this narrative. The first 20% of page one gives a quick overview, and the rest builds a persuasive rationale. The best all-purpose resume, this will work well both at pre-selling and as a leave-behind.

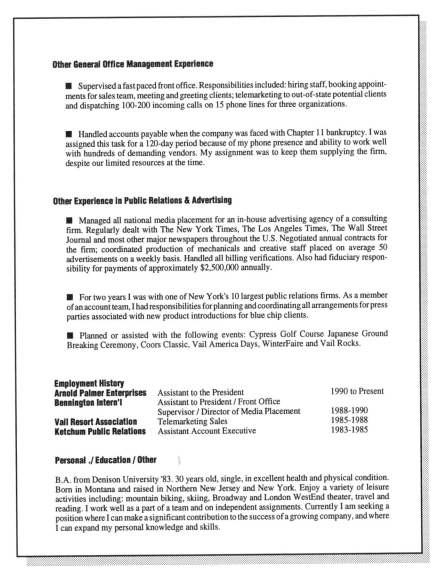

Other General Office Management Experience

■ Supervised a fast paced front office. Responsibilities included: hiring staff, booking appointments for sales team, meeting and greeting clients; telemarketing to out-of-state potential clients and dispatching 100-200 incoming calls on 15 phone lines for three organizations.

■ Handled accounts payable when the company was faced with Chapter 11 bankruptcy. I was assigned this task for a 120-day period because of my phone presence and ability to work well with hundreds of demanding vendors. My assignment was to keep them supplying the firm, despite our limited resources at the time.

Other Experience in Public Relations & Advertising

■ Managed all national media placement for an in-house advertising agency of a consulting firm. Regularly dealt with The New York Times, The Los Angeles Times, The Wall Street Journal and most other major newspapers throughout the U.S. Negotiated annual contracts for the firm; coordinated production of mechanicals and creative staff placed on average 50 advertisements on a weekly basis. Handled all billing verifications. Also had fiduciary responsibility for payments of approximately $2,500,000 annually.

■ For two years I was with one of New York's 10 largest public relations firms. As a member of an account team, I had responsibilities for planning and coordinating all arrangements for press parties associated with new product introductions for blue chip clients.

■ Planned or assisted with the following events: Cypress Golf Course Japanese Ground Breaking Ceremony, Coors Classic, Vail America Days, WinterFaire and Vail Rocks.

Employment History

Arnold Palmer Enterprises	Assistant to the President	1990 to Present
Bennington Intern'l	Assistant to President / Front Office	
	Supervisor / Director of Media Placement	1988-1990
Vail Resort Association	Telemarketing Sales	1985-1988
Ketchum Public Relations	Assistant Account Executive	1983-1985

Personal ./ Education / Other

B.A. from Denison University '83. 30 years old, single, in excellent health and physical condition. Born in Montana and raised in Northern New Jersey and New York. Enjoy a variety of leisure activities including: mountain biking, skiing, Broadway and London WestEnd theater, travel and reading. I work well as a part of a team and on independent assignments. Currently I am seeking a position where I can make a significant contribution to the success of a growing company, and where I can expand my personal knowledge and skills.

"Creative" resume— in narrative style

Not everyone needs this style. It can be very effective in industries where creativity is valued. Here you need a more distinctive "look" than the resume for traditional firms, and allow room for a handwritten note.

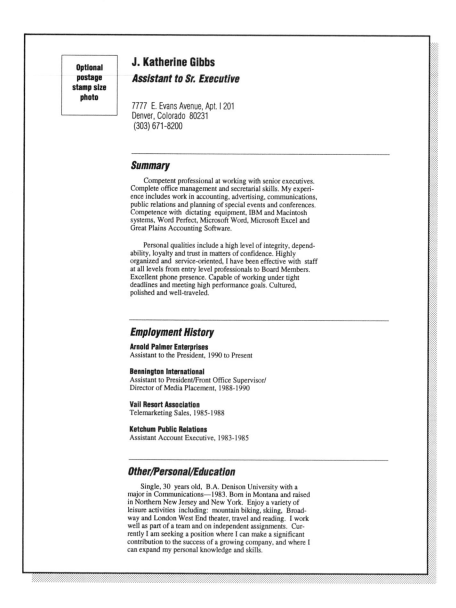

Optional
postage
stamp size
photo

J. Katherine Gibbs

Assistant to Sr. Executive

7777 E. Evans Avenue, Apt. I 201
Denver, Colorado 80231
(303) 671-8200

Summary

Competent professional at working with senior executives. Complete office management and secretarial skills. My experience includes work in accounting, advertising, communications, public relations and planning of special events and conferences. Competence with dictating equipment, IBM and Macintosh systems, Word Perfect, Microsoft Word, Microsoft Excel and Great Plains Accounting Software.

Personal qualities include a high level of integrity, dependability, loyalty and trust in matters of confidence. Highly organized and service-oriented, I have been effective with staff at all levels from entry level professionals to Board Members. Excellent phone presence. Capable of working under tight deadlines and meeting high performance goals. Cultured, polished and well-traveled.

Employment History

Arnold Palmer Enterprises
Assistant to the President, 1990 to Present

Bennington International
Assistant to President/Front Office Supervisor/
Director of Media Placement, 1988-1990

Vail Resort Association
Telemarketing Sales, 1985-1988

Ketchum Public Relations
Assistant Account Executive, 1983-1985

Other/Personal/Education

Single, 30 years old, B.A. Denison University with a major in Communications—1983. Born in Montana and raised in Northern New Jersey and New York. Enjoy a variety of leisure activities including: mountain biking, skiing, Broadway and London West End theater, travel and reading. I work well as part of a team and on independent assignments. Currently I am seeking a position where I can make a significant contribution to the success of a growing company, and where I can expand my personal knowledge and skills.

You can't go wild here or you will leave the impression that you're overselling. The best compromise is to be creative yet professional; low-key but with a different look. Written notes on the first page always get read!

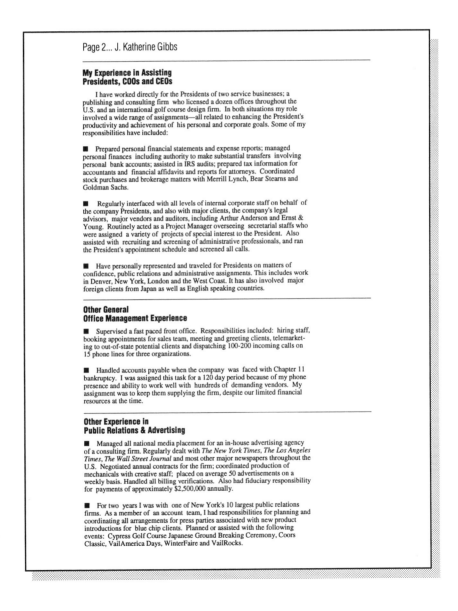

Page 2... J. Katherine Gibbs

My Experience in Assisting Presidents, COOs and CEOs

I have worked directly for the Presidents of two service businesses; a publishing and consulting firm who licensed a dozen offices throughout the U.S. and an international golf course design firm. In both situations my role involved a wide range of assignments—all related to enhancing the President's productivity and achievement of his personal and corporate goals. Some of my responsibilities have included:

■ Prepared personal financial statements and expense reports; managed personal finances including authority to make substantial transfers involving personal bank accounts; assisted in IRS audits; prepared tax information for accountants and financial affidavits and reports for attorneys. Coordinated stock purchases and brokerage matters with Merrill Lynch, Bear Stearns and Goldman Sachs.

■ Regularly interfaced with all levels of internal corporate staff on behalf of the company Presidents, and also with major clients, the company's legal advisors, major vendors and auditors, including Arthur Anderson and Ernst & Young. Routinely acted as a Project Manager overseeing secretarial staffs who were assigned a variety of projects of special interest to the President. Also assisted with recruiting and screening of administrative professionals, and ran the President's appointment schedule and screened all calls.

■ Have personally represented and traveled for Presidents on matters of confidence, public relations and administrative assignments. This includes work in Denver, New York, London and the West Coast. It has also involved major foreign clients from Japan as well as English speaking countries.

Other General Office Management Experience

■ Supervised a fast paced front office. Responsibilities included: hiring staff, booking appointments for sales team, meeting and greeting clients, telemarketing to out-of-state potential clients and dispatching 100-200 incoming calls on 15 phone lines for three organizations.

■ Handled accounts payable when the company was faced with Chapter 11 bankruptcy. I was assigned this task for a 120 day period because of my phone presence and ability to work well with hundreds of demanding vendors. My assignment was to keep them supplying the firm, despite our limited financial resources at the time.

Other Experience in Public Relations & Advertising

■ Managed all national media placement for an in-house advertising agency of a consulting firm. Regularly dealt with *The New York Times*, *The Los Angeles Times*, *The Wall Street Journal* and most other major newspapers throughout the U.S. Negotiated annual contracts for the firm; coordinated production of mechanicals with creative staff; placed on average 50 advertisements on a weekly basis. Handled all billing verifications. Also had fiduciary responsibility for payments of approximately $2,500,000 annually.

■ For two years I was with one of New York's 10 largest public relations firms. As a member of an account team, I had responsibilities for planning and coordinating all arrangements for press parties associated with new product introductions for blue chip clients. Planned or assisted with the following events: Cypress Golf Course Japanese Ground Breaking Ceremony, Coors Classic, VailAmerica Days, WinterFaire and VailRocks.

"Networking" resume— in narrative style

This will work better for getting referrals. The goal of this "look" is to help readers recall your name, and then send a copy to someone who might use your talents. A light first page with room for a handwritten note is essential.

Optional
postage
stamp size
photo

J. Katherine Gibbs
7777 E. Evans Avenue, Apt. I 201
Denver, Colorado 80231
(303) 671-8200

J. Katherine Gibbs

Assistant to Sr. Executive/
Executive Secretary/
Office Management

Summary

Competent professional at working with senior executives. Complete office management and secretarial skills. My experience includes work in accounting, advertising, communications, public relations and planning of special events and conferences. Competence with dictating equipment, IBM and Macintosh systems, Word Perfect, Microsoft Word, Microsoft Excel and Great Plains Accounting Software.

Personal qualities include a high level of integrity, dependability, loyalty and trust in matters of confidence. Highly organized and service-oriented, I have been effective with staff at all levels from entry level professionals to Board Members. Excellent phone presence. Capable of working under tight deadlines and meeting high performance goals. Cultured, polished and well-traveled.

Employment History

Arnold Palmer Enterprises
Assistant to the President, 1990 to Present

Bennington International
Assistant to President/Front Office Supervisor/
Director of Media Placement, 1988-1990

Vail Resort Association
Telemarketing Sales, 1985-1988

Ketchum Public Relations
Assistant Account Executive, 1983-1985

People who receive this won't have jobs for you, so you must use a light front page and a brief summary. The size of the name can vary, but a written note is essential. *"Mr. Jones, you may not recall when we met on United Airlines, but I'll be moving to Dallas and thought you might know of someone ..."*

Page 2... J. Katherine Gibbs

My Experience in Assisting Presidents, COOs and CEOs

I have worked directly for the Presidents of two service businesses; a publishing and consulting firm who licensed a dozen offices throughout the U.S. and an international golf course design firm. In both situations my role involved a wide range of assignments—all related to enhancing the President's productivity and achievement of his personal and corporate goals. Some of my responsibilities have included:

■ Prepared personal financial statements and expense reports; managed personal finances including authority to make substantial transfers involving personal bank accounts; assisted in IRS audits; prepared tax information for accountants and financial affidavits and reports for attorneys. Coordinated stock purchases and brokerage matters with Merrill Lynch, Bear Stearns and Goldman Sachs.

■ Routinely acted as a Project Manager overseeing secretarial staffs who were assigned a variety of projects of special interest to the President. Also assisted with recruiting and screening of administrative professionals, and ran the President's appointment schedule and screened all calls.

■ Regularly interfaced with all levels of internal corporate staff on behalf of the company Presidents, and also with major clients, the company's legal advisors, major vendors and auditors, including Arthur Anderson and Ernst & Young.

■ Have personally represented and traveled for Presidents on matters of confidence, public relations and administrative assignments. This includes work in Denver, New York, London and the West Coast. It has also involved major foreign clients from Japan as well as English speaking countries.

Other General Office Management Experience

■ Supervised a fast paced front office. Responsibilities included: hiring staff, booking appointments for sales team, meeting and greeting clients, telemarketing to out-of-state potential clients and dispatching 100-200 incoming calls on 15 phone lines for three organizations.

■ Handled accounts payable when the company was faced with Chapter 11 bankruptcy. I was assigned this task for a 120 day period because of my phone presence and ability to work well with hundreds of demanding vendors. My assignment was to keep them supplying the firm, despite our limited financial resources at the time.

Other Experience in Public Relations & Advertising

■ Managed all national media placement for an in-house advertising agency of a consulting firm. Regularly dealt with *The New York Times*, *The Los Angeles Times*, *The Wall Street Journal* and most other major newspapers throughout the U.S. Negotiated annual contracts for the firm; coordinated production of mechanicals with creative staff; placed on average 50 advertisements on a weekly basis. Handled all billing verifications. Also had fiduciary responsibility for payments of approximately $2,500,000 annually.

■ For two years I was with one of New York's 10 largest public relations firms. As a member of an account team, I had responsibilities for planning and coordinating all arrangements for press parties associated with new product introductions for blue chip clients.

■ Planned or assisted with the following events: Cypress Golf Course Japanese Ground Breaking Ceremony, Coors Classic, VailAmerica Days, WinterFaire and VailRocks.

■ Responsible for scheduling and planning in state/out of state client conference nationwide for the president, including coordinating meeting dates and location with the clients, securing meeting space, working with hotel sales and catering managers, preparing presentation materials, and making travel arrangements.

Personal/ Education/Other

30 years old, single, in excellent health and physical condition. Willing to travel or relocate. B.A. from Denison University '83. Born in Montana and raised in Northern New Jersey and New York. Enjoy a variety of leisure activities including: mountain biking, skiing, Broadway and London West End theater, travel and reading. I work well as part of a team and on independent assignments. Currently I am seeking a position where I can make a significant contribution to the success of a growing company, and where I can expand my personal knowledge and skills.

"One-page" resumes— in narrative style

With the exception of executives, use one-page resumes for contacting high-volume receivers of resumes such as agencies and associations. To work best, they must have a unique "look." Here are two versions with the same words.

J. Katherine Gibbs
7777 E. Evans Avenue, Apt. I 201 • Denver, Colorado 80231 • (303) 671-8200

Assistant to Sr. Executive/ Executive Secretary/ Office Management

Competent professional at working for senior executives. Complete office management and secretarial skills. My experience includes work in accounting, advertising, communications, public relations and planning of special events and conferences. Competence with dictating equipment, IBM and Macintosh systems, Word Perfect, Microsoft Word, Microsoft Excel and Great Plains Accounting Software.

Personal qualities include a high level of integrity, dependability, loyalty and trust in matters of confidence. Highly organized and service-oriented, I have been effective with staff at all levels from entry level professionals to Board Members. Excellent phone presence. Capable of working under tight deadlines and meeting high performance goals. Cultured, polished and well-traveled.

My Experience in Assisting Presidents, COOs and CEOs

I have worked directly for the Presidents of two service businesses; a publishing and consulting firm who licensed a dozen offices throughout the U.S. and an international golf course design firm. In both situations my role involved a wide range of assignments—all related to enhancing the President's productivity and achievement of his personal and corporate goals. Some of my responsibilities have included:

■ Prepared personal financial statements and expense reports; managed personal finances including authority to make substantial transfers involving personal bank accounts; assisted in IRS audits; prepared tax information for accountants and financial affidavits and reports for attorneys. Coordinated stock purchases and brokerage matters with Merrill Lynch, Bear Stearns and Goldman Sachs.

■ Routinely acted as a Project Manager overseeing secretarial staffs who were assigned a variety of projects of special interest to the President. Also assisted with recruiting and screening of administrative professionals, and ran the President's appointment schedule and screened all calls.

■ Regularly interfaced with all levels of internal corporate staff on behalf of the company Presidents, and also with major clients, the company's legal advisors, major vendors and auditors, including Arthur Anderson and Ernst & Young.

■ Have personally represented and traveled for Presidents on matters of confidence, public relations and administrative assignments. This includes work in Denver, New York, London and the West Coast. It has also involved major foreign clients from Japan as well as English speaking countries.

Other General Office Management Experience

■ Supervised a fast paced front office. Responsibilities included: hiring staff, booking appointments for sales team, meeting and greeting clients, telemarketing to out-of-state potential clients and dispatching 100-200 incoming calls on 15 phone lines for three organizations.

■ Handled accounts payable when the company was faced with Chapter 11 bankruptcy. I was assigned this task for a 120 day period because of my phone presence and ability to work well with hundreds of demanding vendors. My assignment was to keep them supplying the firm, despite our limited financial resources at the time.

Other Experience in Public Relations & Advertising

■ Managed all national media placement for an in-house advertising agency of a consulting firm. Regularly dealt with *The New York Times, The Los Angeles Times, The Wall Street Journal* and most other major newspapers throughout the U.S. Negotiated annual contracts for the firm; coordinated production of mechanicals with creative staff; placed on average 50 advertisements on a weekly basis. Handled all billing verifications. Also had fiduciary responsibility for payments of approximately $2,500,000 annually.

■ For two years I was with one of New York's 10 largest public relations firms. As a member of an account team, I had responsibilities for planning and coordinating all arrangements for press parties associated with new product introductions for blue chip clients.

■ Planned or assisted with the following events: Cypress Golf Course Japanese Ground Breaking Ceremony, Coors Classic, VailAmerica Days, WinterFaire and VailRocks.

■ Responsible for scheduling and planning in state/out of state client conference nationwide for the president, including coordinating meeting dates and location with the clients, securing meeting space, working with hotel sales and catering managers, preparing presentation materials, and making travel arrangements.

Employment History

Arnold Palmer Enterprises
Assistant to the President, 1990 to Present

Bennington International
Assistant to President/Front Office Supervisor/Director of Media Placement, 1988-1990

Vail Resort Association
Telemarketing Sales, 1985-1988

Ketchum Public Relations
Assistant Account Executive, 1983-1985

Other/Personal/ Education

Single, 30 years old, willing to travel or relocate. B.A. Denison University with a major in Communications—1983. Born in Montana and raised in Northern New Jersey and New York. Enjoy a variety of leisure activities including: mountain biking, skiing, Broadway and London West End theater, travel and reading. I work well as part of a team and on independent assignments. Currently I am seeking a position where I can make a significant contribution to the success of a growing company, and where I can expand my personal knowledge and skills.

One-page resumes require a distinctive look. In the rush to present readers with a short resume, most people tell only half their story and it isn't convincing! Both of these examples contain the same full story as the previous examples.

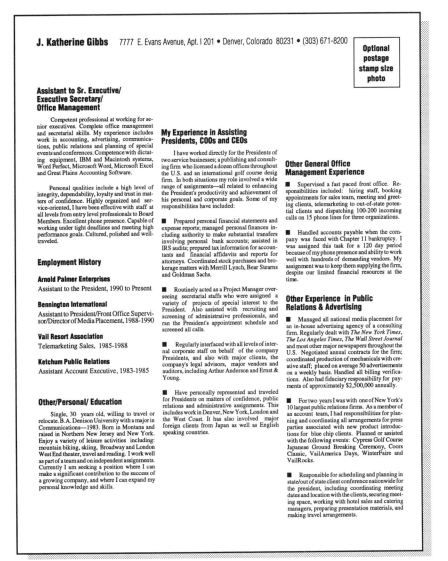

J. Katherine Gibbs   7777 E. Evans Avenue, Apt. I 201 • Denver, Colorado 80231 • (303) 671-8200

Optional postage stamp size photo

Assistant to Sr. Executive/
Executive Secretary/
Office Management

Competent professional at working for senior executives. Complete office management and secretarial skills. My experience includes work in accounting, advertising, communications, public relations and planning of special events and conferences. Competence with dictating equipment, IBM and Macintosh systems, Word Perfect, Microsoft Word, Microsoft Excel and Great Plains Accounting Software.

Personal qualities include a high level of integrity, dependability, loyalty and trust in matters of confidence. Highly organized and service-oriented, I have been effective with staff at all levels from entry level professionals to Board Members. Excellent phone presence. Capable of working under tight deadlines and meeting high performance goals. Cultured, polished and well-traveled.

Employment History

Arnold Palmer Enterprises
Assistant to the President, 1990 to Present

Bennington International
Assistant to President/Front Office Supervisor/Director of Media Placement, 1988-1990

Vail Resort Association
Telemarketing Sales, 1985-1988

Ketchum Public Relations
Assistant Account Executive, 1983-1985

Other/Personal/ Education

Single, 30 years old, willing to travel or relocate. B.A. Denison University with a major in Communications—1983. Born in Montana and raised in Northern New Jersey and New York. Enjoy a variety of leisure activities including: mountain biking, skiing, Broadway and London West End theater, travel and reading. I work well as part of a team and on independent assignments. Currently I am seeking a position where I can make a significant contribution to the success of a growing company, and where I can expand my personal knowledge and skills.

My Experience in Assisting Presidents, COOs and CEOs

I have worked directly for the Presidents of two service businesses; a publishing and consulting firm who licensed a dozen offices throughout the U.S. and an international golf course desig firm. In both situations my role involved a wide range of assignments—all related to enhancing the President's productivity and achievement of his personal and corporate goals. Some of my responsibilities have included:

■ Prepared personal financial statements and expense reports; managed personal finances including authority to make substantial transfers involving personal bank accounts; assisted in IRS audits; prepared tax information for accountants and financial affidavits and reports for attorneys. Coordinated stock purchases and brokerage matters with Merrill Lynch, Bear Stearns and Goldman Sachs.

■ Routinely acted as a Project Manager overseeing secretarial staffs who were assigned a variety of projects of special interest to the President. Also assisted with recruiting and screening of administrative professionals, and ran the President's appointment schedule and screened all calls.

■ Regularly interfaced with all levels of internal corporate staff on behalf of the company Presidents, and also with major clients, the company's legal advisors, major vendors and auditors, including Arthur Anderson and Ernst & Young.

■ Have personally represented and traveled for Presidents on matters of confidence, public relations and administrative assignments. This includes work in Denver, New York, London and the West Coast. It has also involved major foreign clients from Japan as well as English speaking countries.

Other General Office Management Experience

■ Supervised a fast paced front office. Responsibilities included: hiring staff, booking appointments for sales team, meeting and greeting clients, telemarketing to out-of-state potential clients and dispatching 100-200 incoming calls on 15 phone lines for three organizations.

■ Handled accounts payable when the company was faced with Chapter 11 bankruptcy. I was assigned this task for a 120 day period because of my phone presence and ability to work well with hundreds of demanding vendors. My assignment was to keep them supplying the firm, despite our limited financial resources at the time.

Other Experience in Public Relations & Advertising

■ Managed all national media placement for an in-house advertising agency of a consulting firm. Regularly dealt with *The New York Times, The Los Angeles Times, The Wall Street Journal* and most other major newspapers throughout the U.S. Negotiated annual contracts for the firm; coordinated production of mechanicals with creative staff; placed on average 50 advertisements on a weekly basis. Handled all billing verifications. Also had fiduciary responsibility for payments of approximately $2,500,000 annually.

■ For two years I was with one of New York's 10 largest public relations firms. As part of an account team, I had responsibilities for planning and coordinating all arrangements for press parties associated with new product introductions for blue chip clients. Planned or assisted with the following events: Cypress Golf Course Japanese Ground Breaking Ceremony, Coors Classic, VailAmerica Days, WinterFaire and VailRocks.

■ Responsible for scheduling and planning in state/out of state client conference nationwide for the president, including coordinating meeting dates and location with the clients, securing meeting space, working with hotel sales and catering managers, preparing presentation materials, and making travel arrangements.

Let's now discuss an easy six-step system for helping you draft your own superior narrative resumes.

- ❑ Select the right format and lay out the framework
- ❑ Write your objective
- ❑ Write a short summary
- ❑ Write your work experience
- ❑ Let personality show through
- ❑ Make your resume the best it can be

First— select the right resume format and framework

Your starting point is to select the resume format which is best for you. Resume formats offer different ways for arranging your background.

There are four standard resume formats. They include the historical format, the situation format, the achievement format, and the functional format which can emphasize skills or functions.

Your choice will depend on which assets or skills you wish to emphasize and which liabilities you need to downplay. Before you get started, make sure you are familiar with each one. Samples of each format are included in the back of this discussion, along with some advice on who should use them.

Once you've reviewed and decided on a format, you can lay out the framework for your resume. This means putting the headings and subheadings in place.

When you reach the stage to begin writing, don't forget to borrow the phrases from the samples and draw upon what you have surfaced about yourself from our discussion on building an appeal beyond your credentials.

Regardless of the format you've selected, your resume should normally include your objective, a summary of your main selling points, and a strong reinforcing description of your experience and accomplishments.

Second— put your objective at the top of your resume

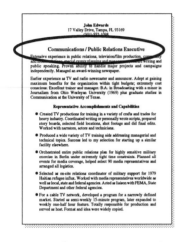

This tells the reader that you are a person with clear purpose, and it enables an employer to quickly assess you in terms of positions that may be available.

Your objective should appear at the top of page one — immediately after your name and address. You may choose to focus on one or more titles or functions.

Regardless of your choice, they should relate to jobs that really exist. For example, "Controller... Assistant Controller," or you may choose to communicate one or more functions if that is more suitable, e.g., "Production Control — Quality Assurance."

For persons with broader objectives a short paragraph may be used. For example, "Qualified as VP of Manufacturing for a medium-sized company or Director of Operations for a large firm."

Or, use a broad functional umbrella with a variety of alternative assignments suggested to a potential employer. For example: *Knowledge of advertising, sales promotion, public relations or product management.*

Third— put a short summary right after your objective

Many of the people who are going to receive your resume will initially glance at it for less than twenty seconds. That's why you need a summary of your most attractive assets to appear early in your resume.

This section may emphasize positive information on any aspect of your story, although most people will want to describe only work experience, education and their most important personal assets. Having an objective and a summary will help ensure that your main selling points will almost always be read. For example.

General Manager— International Operations

Broad experience in international operations, both in large corporations and in start-up situations. Over the past ten years, I have traveled to most world capitals developing client relationships, negotiating acquisitions and making strategic trade decisions involving hundreds of millions of dollars. My educational background includes an MS in Management Science from the University of Chicago plus a BA degree from Denison. Fluent in German, French and English.

Fourth—write an interesting story of your work experience

Personalize your writing with a conversational tone. Dramatize what you can offer and back it up with substance. Recent experience is what really counts.

For credibility, describe the product, industry and market knowledge you've acquired. List positions you held with a given employer — as long as your titles show a pattern of advancement. With average titles use an upgraded term to reference them, e.g. "office management" instead of "administrative assistant."

If you have had an excessive list of jobs, trim or combine the list and emphasize only the key situations. Also, use full descriptions rather than abbreviations.

Too often, people understate their contributions or give all of the credit to someone else. Take credit for larger achievements when you have played a role in the overall effort. Try to quantify your achievements and measure them against some standard, i.e., annually, nationally, percentages, dollar increase or savings, etc.

It can also be helpful to include a brief description of your employer's overall success (in terms of growth rate, revenue, profits, etc.) and a description of their products and services.

Fifth— let your personality show through

Build a positive bridge to people by surfacing a common interest. For example, mention any interest in sports (sailing, skiing, jogging, etc.), or such things as travel experience, military background, home management, club memberships, awards, and hobbies such as photography, music, etc.

Present yourself as more interesting than your competition. You may also want to comment on issues that have potential emotional appeal. For example, commitment, values, motivation, professionalism, reputation, work style, interpersonal skills, among others.

List all degrees completed, as well as any educational credentials that are pending. Include training obtained through military schools, company-sponsored courses, workshops and seminars, or evening courses.

For recent graduates, good grades, part-time work, elected offices, team sports, awards, fraternity or sorority involvements, and leadership experiences can all be included.

Remember, getting some genuine feeling for your personality should be easy for you to do. Phrases that can set you apart appear in the pages that follow this discussion.

Sixth— make your final resume the best it can be

Be attentive to details. Factors such as paper, margins and spacing, along with type size, style and layout must be considered.

❏ Have you chosen the right format— one that allows you to sell assets and minimize liabilities?

❏ Is your objective clear and the resume distinctive and appealing?

❏ Does the summary present your best selling points?

❏ Do the sentences flow smoothly?

❏ Is your story persuasive?

❏ Check your grammar. People discard resumes because of grammar or the fact that they are too hard to read.

❏ Some experts will tell you never to use a picture, but small postage-stamp-size photographs work very well. People prefer to invite applicants whose picture they have seen for an interview.

You don't need to look like a model to use a photo this size. The qualities to convey are that you are pleasant, friendly, easy to get along with, clean cut and trustworthy. In short–someone who would be a credit to the firm. Consider having a friend shoot a roll of 36 on 35 mm color film, make a contact sheet and select the best photo.

A special note for professionals who just might change more than once

Remember the old expression KYRTD. It's been around for some time and stands for "Keep Your Resume Up-To-Date." Well, today, it's better advice than ever before.

One of the best things you can do for yourself and your career is to always have an updated narrative available and on hand. I know of few professionals at any level who would not benefit from this and who just might find it the key to a terrific future position.

As you go through your career, you're likely to become aware of dozens of attractive opportunities, but rarely will you be able to capitalize on them at the moment. If you make an effort, but you lack a superior biography, you will be handicapped by material that just doesn't cut it.

The kinds of situations I'm referring to include the occasional call from a recruiter, the opening that's come up with a competitor that is a level or two above where you are, the absolutely ideal ad you happen to see, the friend who tells you about an upcoming opportunity. I could go on, but I'm sure you've got the idea.

Your key to being able to respond fast and get consideration will often rest squarely with your ability to quickly supply a low-key but highly persuasive background summary about yourself— one that seemingly was drafted in a couple of days— and just for the person who requested it!

So, develop an excellent narrative for yourself. Then, work it until it tells just the right story. Keep it on disk and update it from time to time. It just might make the difference.

As you write your resume here are some key phrases that can be powerful

- ❑ Managed a very successful _____.
- ❑ Earned the _____ award at _____.
- ❑ Ranked number _____ in sales for _____ years.
- ❑ Planned, managed and supervised events for up to _____ people.
- ❑ Completed assignments to our clients' complete satisfaction.
- ❑ Proven ability to get team members into action.
- ❑ Succeeded in only _____ months to educate myself in _____ areas.
- ❑ Outstanding record in recruiting, training and motivating employees.
- ❑ Successfully published _____ in (local), (regional) or (national) media.
- ❑ Designed and implemented a highly successful employee _____.
- ❑ Designed courses to train over _____ people.
- ❑ Proven track record of designing and implementing successful projects.
- ❑ Strongly self-motivated, enthusiastic and profit-oriented.
- ❑ Thrive on working with people and helping clients achieve their objectives.
- ❑ Highly motivated and goal-oriented.
- ❑ High energy coupled with enthusiasm and dedication to _____.
- ❑ Enthusiastic, creative and willing to assume increased responsibility.
- ❑ Long-term interest in _____.
- ❑ Unique abilities to help others.
- ❑ Well-versed in _____. A generator of creative ideas.
- ❑ An innovative trainer and educator.
- ❑ A quick learner with ability to adapt to new challenges.
- ❑ A creative flair for putting on events.
- ❑ Exceptionally adept at handling complex matters.
- ❑ Unusual talent for creating solutions which are commercially successful.
- ❑ A life-long exposure to ____. Strong affiliation with _____.
- ❑ Familiar with _____ cultures and politics.
- ❑ Long-term exposure to _____ business.
- ❑ Raised in a family of successful people. Strong work ethic.
- ❑ Strong credentials in ___ and _____.
- ❑ Trained by one of the area's most reputable _____.
- ❑ A licensed _____ with ____ years of professional experience.
- ❑ I've had specialized courses in _____ and _____.
- ❑ Theoretical grounding in _____ and _____.
- ❑ Outstanding communication and presentation skills.
- ❑ Possess a positive, professional image suitable for any business environment.
- ❑ Effective at public speaking and media presentations.
- ❑ Excellent moderator and mediator.
- ❑ Communicate well with a wide range of personalities.
- ❑ Excellent communicator; able to draw people out and quickly put them at ease.
- ❑ Skilled at interpreting complex regulations.
- ❑ Effective negotiator.

- ❏ Excellent written and verbal communication skills.
- ❏ Extensive contacts in the _____ field.
- ❏ Extensive public service in nonprofit organizations.
- ❏ First hand experience with a wide range of cultures.
- ❏ Excellent command of both _____ and _____ languages.
- ❏ Effective in working with people from _____.
- ❏ Extensive experience in negotiating foreign contracts.
- ❏ Successfully opened profitable foreign markets.
- ❏ Able to resolve conflicts in a diplomatic manner.
- ❏ Skilled at developing rapport with all types of people.
- ❏ Ability to bring harmony among diverse groups.
- ❏ Skilled in resolving conflicts where other people failed.
- ❏ Diplomatic and tactful with both professionals and nonprofessionals.
- ❏ Skilled in handling public matters with professionalism.
- ❏ Effectively interfaced with management at all levels.
- ❏ An effective decision-maker. A seasoned professional.
- ❏ Well-organized and resourceful.
- ❏ Extremely dependable in completing projects.
- ❏ Can be counted on to get the job done.
- ❏ Effective independently or as a member of the team.
- ❏ Excellent organization, communication and writing skills.
- ❏ Ability to organize many documents into a coherent presentation.
- ❏ Creative problem solver.
- ❏ Outstanding ability to assess clients' needs.
- ❏ Special talent for improving systems. Able to accurately establish priorities.
- ❏ Able to pinpoint problems and initiate creative solutions.
- ❏ Proven ability to gain customers' confidence.
- ❏ Experienced in developing long-term customer relations.
- ❏ Have inspired the trust of people at all levels.
- ❏ Excellent professional reputation among _____.
- ❏ Excellent references from _____.
- ❏ Enjoy an industry-wide reputation for _____.
- ❏ High level of professionalism.
- ❏ Project a highly competent and professional image.
- ❏ Poised and competent as a professional representative.
- ❏ Personable, articulate and professional in both appearance and manners.
- ❏ Extremely sociable, able to put clients at ease.
- ❏ Special talent for coordinating colors and visual effects.
- ❏ Effective in developing programs which reach goals.
- ❏ Special talent for inspiring creative excellence.
- ❏ A finely tuned sense of _____ and its uses.

❑ Well-versed in _____ laws and regulations.
❑ Familiar with the scope and quality of _____ programming.
❑ Effective in persuading others through enthusiasm for good ideas and products.
❑ Able to maintain a sense of humor.Remain calm under demanding conditions.
❑ Able to handle a multitude of details and meet close deadlines under pressure.
❑ Versatile troubleshooter who can turn around poor performing _____ .
❑ Take pride in achieving the best possible results. Dedicated professional.
❑ Thrive in organizing complex projects.
❑ Thrive on a dynamic and challenging environment.
❑ A self-starter, highly ambitious and goal-directed.
❑ Resourceful and committed— can always be counted on to get the job done.
❑ Consumer-oriented professional who can market high-quality products.
❑ Effective in high-pressure situations.Well-versed in the use of _____ .
❑ Effectively streamlined _____ and reduced _____ by ($, %).
❑ Able to meet and exceed corporate goals.
❑ Headed new products development teams.
❑ Well-versed in establishing distribution networks (nationally) (internationally).
❑ Appointed _____ of _____ committee.
❑ Experienced with highly respected industry-leading firms.
❑ Experienced in a fast-moving growth company. Have led by example.
❑ Skilled at running seminars and conferences.
❑ Ethics and character of the highest caliber.
❑ A skillful negotiator in _____ situations.
❑ Have worked closely with top management.
❑ Have enjoyed success with practical approaches to____situations.
❑ Have been able to inspire others to maximum performance.
❑ Can cut through nonessentials to the heart of problems.
❑ Initiated sweeping changes. Performed against tight deadlines.
❑ Thoroughly familiar with the _____ market.
❑ Have turned around marginal operations in the field.
❑ Have well-developed instincts for what will sell.
❑ Salvaged a previously unprofitable operation in the _____ industry.
❑ Particularly skilled at directing large meetings.
❑ Have been consistently able to turn complaints into manageable situations.
❑ Have coached winning teams.
❑ Have planned and managed fund-raising programs.
❑ Have recruited and trained committed volunteers
❑ Have been able to bring order out of chaos.
❑ Have substantial project management experience.

In the first section of this chapter we covered our preferred style of resumes. Here are some other 2-page narrative resumes that illustrate the most popular resume formats.

Remember, these formats simply offer different ways for arranging your background and presenting information.

"Historical" format— written in narrative style

This outlines your career in chronological order, starting with your most recent employer. The most popular format, it works best for people whose careers include a succession of increasingly responsible positions.

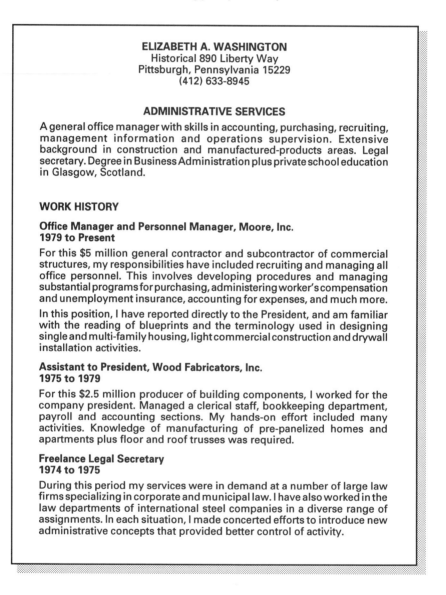

ELIZABETH A. WASHINGTON
Historical 890 Liberty Way
Pittsburgh, Pennsylvania 15229
(412) 633-8945

ADMINISTRATIVE SERVICES

A general office manager with skills in accounting, purchasing, recruiting, management information and operations supervision. Extensive background in construction and manufactured-products areas. Legal secretary. Degree in Business Administration plus private school education in Glasgow, Scotland.

WORK HISTORY

Office Manager and Personnel Manager, Moore, Inc.
1979 to Present

For this $5 million general contractor and subcontractor of commercial structures, my responsibilities have included recruiting and managing all office personnel. This involves developing procedures and managing substantial programs for purchasing, administering worker's compensation and unemployment insurance, accounting for expenses, and much more.

In this position, I have reported directly to the President, and am familiar with the reading of blueprints and the terminology used in designing single and multi-family housing, light commercial construction and drywall installation activities.

Assistant to President, Wood Fabricators, Inc.
1975 to 1979

For this $2.5 million producer of building components, I worked for the company president. Managed a clerical staff, bookkeeping department, payroll and accounting sections. My hands-on effort included many activities. Knowledge of manufacturing of pre-panelized homes and apartments plus floor and roof trusses was required.

Freelance Legal Secretary
1974 to 1975

During this period my services were in demand at a number of large law firms specializing in corporate and municipal law. I have also worked in the law departments of international steel companies in a diverse range of assignments. In each situation, I made concerted efforts to introduce new administrative concepts that provided better control of activity.

ELIZABETH A. WASHINGTON
PAGE 2...

Legal Secretary
1967 to 1974

From 1969 to 1974, I worked for the Senior Partner in a large international law firm in Pittsburgh. My responsibilities involved subsidized housing, public safety, land development and zoning, city and suburban police work. I was also heavily involved in corporate law through my presence at Board meetings where I recorded proceedings.

With Jones, Barry & Miller from 1967 to 1968, I worked on general and corporate law matters and headed a campaign committee for James Miller, a Senior Partner. Judge Miller was successfully elected to the Superior Court of Los Angeles, Orange County, California. Among my other contributions were the critical filing of documents at the recorder's office and research of public records.

EUROPEAN BACKGROUND

Prior to emigrating to America, I was associated with Fleming & Wilson, a firm of Chartered Accountants located in Glasgow, Scotland. My work involved the graphic preparation of profit and loss statements and balance sheets, as well as a substantial amount of statistical typing.

PERSONAL & EDUCATION

My health is excellent. I am married and have one child. My appearance and communication skills are appropriate for any quality business environment. My degree in Business Administration has been supplemented by courses in Business Management, Law, Psychology, Accounting and Human Resources.

My goal is to contribute in a challenging environment where there is a need for a top producer. I am confident that I possess the sensitivity, intelligence and enthusiasm that will assure exceptional results. I would be happy to expand upon this in a personal meeting.

"Functional" format— written in narrative style

This portrays your career according to "business functions" performed (sales, accounting, etc.). It's great for generalists; career changers; homemakers; people who were with one firm a long time; and those who have had too many jobs.

William Cross

168 East 60th St., New York, NY 10022 • 212-726-3463

General Management Executive	Experienced management executive—with a record of over 20 years proven accomplishments in the areas of sales, marketing, personnel, production and purchasing.
	Have handled a wide variety of responsibilities and progressed from Foreman through Vice President. Recently in charge of the complete management of sales & profits for a major division.
	Widely traveled and willing to relocate. Education includes study at the University of California. Military service consisted of 4 years in the U.S. Army (attained rank of Captain).
	Personal attributes include dedication to a job... the ability to effect strong loyalty from subordinates... effectiveness in working independently or as part of a team... capacity to get things done... and the managerial skill to meet stringent production, sales or cost objectives.
Areas of Major Experience	Have been responsible for large-scale work forces— union and nonunion, technical and administrative. Have had full authority for all hiring and termination, the execution of union negotiations and responsibility for salary administration.
Human Resources	Numerous accomplishments in skillfully managing a staff. Proven ability for inspiring loyalty and minimizing absenteeism, turnover and serious labor problems.
Sales & Marketing	Have been responsible for a sales organization which generated a volume of $7,000,000. During a five-year period, sales and profits were tripled. Opened new markets for products through contact on a direct basis with chains.

196

You can use this same functional style and choose to emphasize skills rather than functions. For example your experience and achievements in project management; presentations; analytical assignments; volunteer work; organizing etc.

Page Two... William Cross

Production

Personally developed and introduced sales promotions and associated point-of-purchase materials.

Have strong personal contacts with officers and owners of various chains including such firms as A&P, Jewel Tea, Finast, Safeway, Penn Fruit, etc.

Widely experienced in managing production output and problems. Previous positions held include Production Supervisor and Plant Manager.

Have a record of accomplishments in all of the above positions. Some examples follow:

(1) Frequently overhauled production schedules and coordinated work between shifts to effect significant savings in time, direct labor and overhead costs.
(2) Initiated sweeping quality and product controls which led to superior company performance.
(3) Introduced systems of cost and price controls and insured their useful implementation.

Purchasing

Have been responsible for a wide range of purchasing functions.

Provided input from a purchasing perspective in the design of new plants in major cities. These included facilities for production, warehousing and shipping.

Introduced quality control reports which led to guides for bulk purchasing, and provided guidance to Plant Managers on pricing and inventory controls.

Employment

Complete history and references are available upon the establishment of a mutual interest.

Personal

Married. Enjoy cross country-skiing, musical theater and tournament chess.

"Situation" format— written in narrative style

This format tells a story through journalistic headlines. It gives fast-moving explanations of situations and how you dealt with them. This format can be very effective for executives and others who may be strong generalists.

Paul Carlson
803 Victoria Lane
Arlington Hts., IL 60005
312-693-3917

**General Management/
Sales Executive**

As a 20-year IBM executive, my most recent assignment has been to revitalize a $50,000,000 multi-location activity that employed 815 persons. In a drive to restore profitability, I reversed the downward trend, established a new marketing concept, and eliminated manufacturing bottlenecks in less than six months. In addition to a $4,500,000 gain in profits, revenue advanced by 45%.

Earlier, I held P&L responsibilities as General Manager of a new operation. In this position, my efforts drew praise from top executives throughout our $20-billion corporation. As a result, I was awarded IBM's most prestigious management honor, "The President's Trophy."

Previously, as District Manager in the lowest-ranked GEM district in the nation, I was instrumental in our growth to top position 24 months later... with sales increasing by $50,000,000. Prior assignments included responsibilities as Product Marketing Manager at our $800,000,000 regional headquarters, and as Sales Manager responsible for a 75-man team of engineers and representatives in the Los Angeles area.

Starting in sales, I earned supervisory responsibilities in less than three years. My personal background includes an M.B.A. from Harvard, and a B.A. from Amherst.

I joined IBM in 1970 when the Data Processing Division was still in its infancy. Since then I have participated in one of the most complex expansions ever engineered by a U.S. corporation. A few highlights of my overall career are indicated as follows:

**Revitalization and Expansion
of a $50,000,000 Operation**

In mid-1980, my attention focused on an unusual situation within the company. Headquarters' staff had tentatively decided to discontinue our established operations. Both revenue ($50,000,000) and profit had been falling for an extended period of time. In spite of their cautions, I promoted the concept of reorganization.

It can also work well for anyone who is relatively short on years of experience, but who can talk about a few key situations they have encountered that build support for their objective.

Page 2... Paul Carlson

Once my plans were approved, I moved rapidly on a number of fronts. At the outset, I reduced the 815-person staff by more than 15%, eliminating duplication of effort in all departments. In addition, I shifted our basic marketing strategy, which allowed us to substantially increase revenue. Then, working closely with our Controller, I tightened controls in all areas. By year end, a full profit recovery was clearly established by more than $4,500,000. Sales had increased 45%.

New Business Start-up
in Los Angeles

As corporate growth continued to accelerate throughout the late 1970s, I was charged with the responsibility for opening a new office in the Los Angeles area. After an exceptionally fast start-up, we entered some of the toughest years ever experienced by the Data Processing Division.

It was against this backdrop that I launched a 5-year plan destined to rank my organization among the top performing offices in the country. We eventually employed 15 managers and more than 100 support personnel, with revenue reaching $33,000,000 per year by 1979. Our consistent ability to meet revenue and expense targets, coupled with long-range planning effectiveness, led to personal performance ratings of "rarely ever achieved."

Building the Northwest Area
of the United States

When appointed as second in command of this $220,000,000 district, it was recognized that sales were not up to expectations. During my 24-month assignment, I coordinated 15 major offices throughout the northwest. My direct responsibilities included marketing, accounts receivable, planning and product objectives, as well as the preparation of sales quotas and special promotions. Additional duties included recruiting, education and resource allocation.

One of our major accomplishments was moving this district from a 7th ranking nationally in 1974, to 1st ranking in 1975. This was an intense effort targeted toward 24 quantitative objectives. By the end of my tenure, we had organized the entire staff into an efficient team-oriented operation.

"Achievement" format— written in narrative style

This format is most commonly used by achievers and people whose main accomplishments may not be in their most recent position. Try to use specific numbers, time frames, and percentages in describing achievements.

John Edwards
17 Valley Drive, Tampa, FL 93169
(301) 552-1098

Communications / Public Relations Executive

Extensive experience in public relations, television/film production, community and media relations, special events planning and management, feature writing and public speaking. Proven ability to handle major projects and campaigns independently. Managed an award-winning newspaper.

Earlier experience as TV and radio newscaster and announcer. Adept at gaining maximum benefits for the organization within tight budgets; extremely cost conscious. Excellent trainer and manager. B.A. in Broadcasting with a minor in Journalism from Ohio Wesleyan University (1969) plus graduate studies in Communication at the University of Texas.

Representative Accomplishments and Capabilities

● Created TV productions for training in a variety of crafts and trades for heavy industry. Coordinated writing or personally wrote scripts, prepared story boards, selected field locations, shot footage and did final edits. Worked with narrators, actors and technicians.

● Produced a wide variety of TV training aids addressing managerial and technical topics. Success led to my selection for starting up a similar facility elsewhere.

● Orchestrated entire public relations plan for highly sensitive military exercise in Berlin under extremely tight time constraints. Planned all events for media coverage, helped select 90 media representatives and arranged all logistics.

● Selected as on-site relations coordinator of military support for 1979 Haitian refugee influx. Worked with media representatives worldwide as well as local, state and federal agencies. Acted as liaison with FEMA, State Department and other federal agencies.

● For a cable TV network, developed a program for a narrowly defined market. Started as semi-weekly 15-minute program, later expanded to weekly one-half hour feature. Totally responsible for production and served as host. Format and idea were widely copied.

Page 2... John Edwards

- As an excellent public speaker, have been selected as Master of Ceremonies and spokesman for many important special events and ceremonies. Chosen as participant in Air Force Systems Command Speakers Bureau, a select marketing and public relations group.

- Produced audio feature package for Saturn launch. Produced three TV clips for networks covering the recovery forces for Saturn. Managed Department of Defense news desk at the NASA Press Center for both Pluto and Saturn. Developed excellent press kits.

- Revitalized and managed a recorded news service for radio stations, enabling them to call in and get "beeper" reports on a variety of U.S. Air Force issues and topics.

- As a freelance writer, have been widely published in a variety of national magazines, including "EMT Gazette," "Paddleball" and "Compass," the military public affairs magazine. Have had photo features published in "Karate Sphere" and "Undersea."

Employment History

Atlantic Eastern Video Concepts	1983 to Present
Television Producer	
U.S. Air Force	1970 to 1983
Public Affairs Plans Officer	1980 to 1983
Public Affairs Staff Officer	1979 to 1983
Deputy Chief of Information	1976 to 1979
Director of Operations	1976 to 1979
Chief of Information	1974 to 1976
Information Officer	1972 to 1974
TV Production Officer	1970 to 1972

Personal

A former member of the River End Public Relations Society and the Foreign Correspondents Club of China. Active in the community as a Scout leader (former Eagle Scout) and as a volunteer Cardiac Emergency Medical Technician for Norfolk, Virginia (two terms on Board of Directors). Leisure activities include photography, scuba diving, amateur radio, racquetball, theater and travel. Married and in excellent health. Willing to travel and would consider relocation for the right opportunity.

There is nothing like using letters that are carefully customized for each audience you contact. If you have the time, they will almost always produce more interviews than sending resumes with cover letters.

The ten most common letters that you may need in your job search

Once you have written your narrative resumes, it is very easy to prepare all the letters you might require. Here are the ten most common letters that people need to use as part of a comprehensive job search. On the pages that follow you will find a range of letter samples. They can be easily modified and adapted to your own situation.

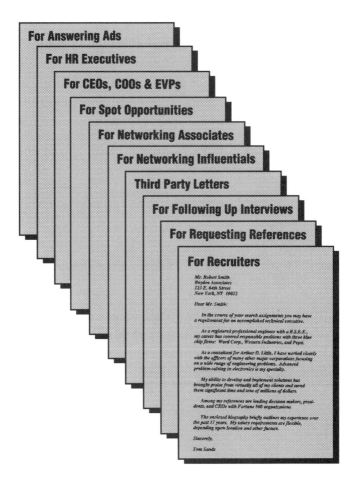

For answering ads

Mr. Dale Perkins
Vice President, Sales
Microsoft Corporation
1 Microsoft Way
Redmond, WA 98052

Dear Mr. Perkins:

I was quite struck by your ad for a Regional Sales Manager. My qualifications seem to be a perfect fit.

As a District Sales Manager, I set up a branch office for a company in the office products industry. Under my leadership, sales increased 23% and 58% respectively in the first two years of operation.

I believe I could do as well for you... and I'd like to try. My immediate interest is in obtaining a Regional Sales Manager's position that offers superior potential for a young person who can prove her value to Microsoft.

My background also includes administrative and supervisory responsibilities in the areas of hiring, training and motivating people.

I'm single, 29 years old and have a B.A. degree from Indiana University. There I was elected Student Body President and graduated third in my class.

May I have the opportunity to further discuss my qualifications during a personal interview? A more detailed summary of my background is attached. I would look forward to speaking with you and will call your secretary on Wednesday to see if something convenient for you can be arranged.

Sincerely,

Lynn Reilly

For human resource executives

Mr. Michael Walters
Vice President, Human Resources
Coca Cola of America, Inc.
1 Coca Cola Plaza NW
Atlanta, GA 30313

Dear Mr. Walters:

For a number of years I have been associated with a firm which is a major supplier to many subsidiaries of your company. In line with this, I thought you might be able to direct me to appropriate divisional executives with whom I could communicate.

I am an experienced corporation lawyer. My career has spanned a broad range of legal functions involving substantial responsibility and requiring great sensitivity.

Most recently, I assisted in the restructuring of a major company under Chapter XI of the Bankruptcy Act. In reviewing the firm's contract practices, I identified millions of dollars of credits that had been previously unrecognized.

Prior to this, I developed the widely copied Budweiser franchise agreement. It is considered to be the standard against which all other agreements are measured. My education includes a Bachelor of Arts degree from Hobart College and a Law degree from Georgetown University. I am a member of the New York Bar.

I know many areas of your business very well. Furthermore, I want to find a new position where I can make the best use of my expertise. I would appreciate an opportunity to bring my qualifications to the attention of senior executives with Coca Cola who might benefit from my experience. I will call you Monday to see if you can suggest who would be the right people for me to contact.

Sincerely,

Robert Johnson

For CEOs, COOs & VPs

Mr. John Pepper, President
Procter & Gamble Inc.
1 Procter & Gamble Plaza
Cincinnati, OH 45202

Dear Mr. Pepper:

P&G's leading position in the food industry has been of great interest to me for some time. This, along with your well known reputation for attracting the best marketing talent have prompted this letter.

In my current role of a Senior Marketing Manager for General Foods, I recently launched a new breakfast product. I am sure it is familiar to you and it has been successful despite fierce competition. Under my direction, this product initially captured 7% of the market. Within one year our share has risen to 13%, and the brand is now well-poised for additional growth in years ahead.

Having accumulated 9 years of similar successes, I now feel ready to assume broader responsibilities as a Vice President of Marketing. While I am happy with General Foods and have been treated very well, such growth opportunities will not be possible because of organizational reasons. However, recent articles in the press have left me with the sense that my timing may tie in well with your plans.

Of additional importance, I have always had an interest in living in Cincinnati. In fact, last month I spent a wonderful week competing in the Lake Caldor classic. This along with some close friends convinced me that we would like to relocate to your beautiful city in the near future.

On Monday I will call your secretary to see if a convenient meeting can be arranged.

Very truly yours,

Mitch Watson

For spot opportunities

Mr. J. E. Treadway
V.P., Human Resources
R.R. Donnelley Corporation
77 West Wacker Drive
Chicago, IL 60601

Dear Mr. Treadway:

Your company's new emphasis on human resources was highlighted in this month's "Personnel Journal." I enjoyed reading this article and agree with many of the points you made.

As a professional with five years successful experience in HR, I though my expertise in helping accomplish the goals you outlined might be of interest.

In my present position as regional HR director with a $200 million firm, I have had full responsibility for implementing the industrial relations programs at our facilities in Chicago.

Some of my other accomplishments have included

* Designing the corporation's employee manual

* Training HR staff in Dallas, Los Angeles and Seattle

* Helping maintain a level of superior labor relations that has been widely recognized in our industry.

At 34 years of age and married with two children, I have a BA and a MA from Southern Methodist University. Relocation and travel requirements present no problem. Confident that you would find a personal meeting both interesting and mutually profitable, I will call you on Thursday to arrange an interview at your convenience. I look forward to seeing if I can help with the exciting challenges you face.

Very truly yours,

Michael Arnold

For networking associates

Mrs. Lois Palko
19 Spruce Street
North Caldwell, New Jersey 07006

Dear Lois:

It isn't often, unfortunately, that I write letters to old friends. There's a good reason for doing so now and it involves a favor.

As you may know, I have maintained a successful consulting practice over recent years. This has been most rewarding. However, I have recently decided to seek out a new line assignment as President of a small- to medium-size corporation, or as Marketing Executive with a larger firm.

As part of this new direction, I am interested in expanding my circle of acquaintances at the level of CEO. Considering your long history in the area, it seems that you may be able to provide me with a few select introductions in Northern New Jersey.

Ideal contacts would be with Chief Executives with firms having significant growth potential. A company facing a turn-around situation could also be interesting.

In any event, I hope to move swiftly in securing appropriate contacts. If you don't mind, I would like to review some preliminary possibilities with you... situations which may signal the need for a person like myself.

Please give my best regards to Bob. Thanks in advance for your time. I'll give you a ring later in the week.

With my best regards,

Gordon Edwards

For networking influential people

Mr. Frank V. Cahouet
President, Mellon Bank
1 Mellon Bank Center
Pittsburgh, PA 15258

Dear Mr. Cahouet:

As President of Mellon Bank and a person well-known in financial circles, you have unique insight into firms throughout the state. That is the reason for this letter.

My most recent executive assignment has been as Chief Financial Officer of Carter Products, Inc., a $60,000,000 producer of furniture. In that position, my achievements contributed heavily to the following results:

A major profit decline was reversed as our earnings have jumped 30% within 2 years.

A complete reorganization was put into effect and a brand new EDP system was successfully installed.

Earlier, I held increasingly responsible positions with the Henredon.

Now, after careful thought, I have decided to seek out new opportunities in Pittsburgh. Therefore, I am taking the liberty of enclosing a brief resume.

Mr. Cahouet, if you could spare fifteen minutes sometime next week, I would enjoy the opportunity to speak with you briefly. With that in mind, I will call your secretary next Tuesday to see what might be arranged.

Sincerely,

Paul Williams

Using a third-party

Mr. James Miller
Sr. Vice President, Chrysler Corporation
12000 Chrysler Drive
Highland Park, Michigan 48288

Dear Mr. Miller:

A close business associate has asked me to contact you on his behalf. Recently, he noted the Business Week article about the merger that you have just completed.

Now that the dust has settled, perhaps the need for an Executive with a management background has arisen. If this is the case, I believe he may be someone you should talk to.

His early experience was with Ford, where he progressed rapidly through their manufacturing functions. As I recall, their processes still make use of many of his innovations.

In 1986 after 8 years at Ford, he moved to another large manufacturing company. While there, he further refined his management skills, becoming VP-Operations.

The company has now returned to profitability as a result of his effort. He is ready to take on new challenges which match his ability as a top performer.

In light of your acquisition, he indicated a real interest in meeting you. I would recommend that you review the enclosed resume. If you then have an interest, I can arrange for a meeting with you at a mutually convenient time.

Sincerely,

Tom Donaldson

For following up an interview

Mr. Richard D. McCormick, President
U S West Corporation
7800 E. Orchard Ave.
Englewood, Colorado 80111

Dear Mr. McCormick:

I just wanted to say how much I enjoyed our conversation on Monday afternoon. The Financial Planning position which you described sounded both interesting and challenging.

As I mentioned to you, my previous experience in the area of Financial Planning includes work for both A.T.& T. and the General Electric Company.

While at General Electric, I was the primary force behind the development of the corporation's latest five-year financial plan. If either you or Mr. Wilson are interested, I would be glad to sketch out in more detail the exact accomplishments which I made in this area... and the systems we used.

I will be out of town next week, Mr. McCormick. After that, I certainly hope we can explore things further at your convenience. As previously stated, I am very confident regarding my potential contribution to U S West.

Thank you again for your time.

Sincerely,

Marsha Randall

For requesting references

Dr. Michael Sovern
President, Columbia University
212 Hamilton Hall
New York, NY 10027

Dear Dr. Sovern:

It seems like years since we last talked, but I hope that all is well with you. Since graduating from Columbia University my career has taken some very interesting turns.

For the first three years I worked as an assistant to the public relations director at Merrill Lynch. My earnings there allowed me to finance a graduate degree, which I will be completing this month.

Two years ago I had a unique opportunity come to my attention from the Clairol Corporation. Despite my relatively young age, I now have two years experience as manager of public relations for their largest division.

Unfortunately, it looks as though the company will be sold in the next few months. As part of our impending merger all staff positions will be under review, and this prompts my reason for this letter.

If it is convenient, I would like to use you as a reference in case I do need to consider a new move. To bring you up to date I am attaching a copy of my most recent resume for your review. Any thoughts regarding improvements would be a great help.

I will give you a ring on Tuesday and look forward to speaking to you again.

Very truly yours,

Paul Richards

For sending to recruiters

Mr. Russell Reynolds
Russell Reynolds & Associates
200 Park Avenue
New York, N.Y. 10166

Dear Mr. Reynolds:

In the course of your search assignments you may have a requirement for an accomplished technical executive.

As a Registered Professional Engineer with a B.S.E.E., my career has covered responsible positions with three blue chip firms: Conagra, Western Electric, and G.E.

As a consultant, I have worked closely with the officers of many other major corporations focusing on a wide range of engineering problems.

My ability to develop and implement solutions has brought praise from virtually all of my clients and saved them significant time and money.

The enclosed resume briefly outlines my experience over the past 17 years. My salary requirements would be in the area of $55,000 to $65,000, depending upon location and other factors.

If it appears that my qualifications meet the needs of one of your clients, I would be happy to discuss my background further in a meeting with you.

Sincerely,

Roy Baker

For writing memos—just adapt these samples to your personal situation

In a recent article, Arthur Levine made it plain that North Central is a progressive bank which prides itself in attracting "results-oriented" people. I believe the attached resume will show that I fit that description.

Congratulations on your appointment as Vice President Sales! A brief review of the attached resume will indicate a few of the reasons I think that I can be of help.

I thrive on challenges involving cost control and can be very effective in vendor relations. Also, as the attached resume illustrates, I am good at turnaround situations.

Recent news indicates you're expanding in the South. Maybe I can help. As you can see from the attached, I've had five years of solid experience in plant operations. I've also been through start-ups, and they inspire me. I certainly would enjoy talking with you.

If getting results is a primary qualification for this job, the attached resume will indicate that I have consistently demonstrated that ability. I am confident that I can contribute immediately in the position described.

Enthusiasm is an important quality that can be hard to describe. However, it is a quality that I can bring to the position you advertised. I would like to have the opportunity to tell you how my energy, plus five years of experience in your field, can be a winning combination for you.

I have been inspired by the leadership repeatedly demonstrated by your company. I'd like to put my own interest and knowledge to good use for the firm. My background is solid and my interest is strong. May I hear from you?

The position you have described sounds ideally matched to my personal and educational qualifications. On top of that, I can bring you the benefits of years of experience in the industry, and an outstanding record of accomplishments.

My background perfectly matches the qualifications stated in your advertisement. The attached resume will support this. In addition, I am very much interested in your company.

Your company was recommended to me by a friend. He indicated that you have opportunities for recent graduates with my background.

I am seeking a more challenging position. Because your recruiting firm has an excellent reputation, a friend in Human Resources suggested I contact you.

Congratulations on the design breakthrough of the P400. That is the reason for my brief note. The attached resume will tell you about my track record in successfully penetrating markets for three different companies. I can do it for you, too!

Congratulations on your promotion to President. Perhaps you could use a financial assistant with five years experience.

*NOTE: All of these should end with a comment that indicates when you will follow up on your correspondence. For example, "I will call you next Tuesday to see when something convenient can be arranged."

Section Four: Interviewing & Negotiating

Getting the right interviews is only half the battle. This next section will help you convert them into attractive offers. As a general rule, most people require between six and ten interviews to develop a single offer.

I realize that entire books have been written on these subjects. However, the next two chapters on interviewing and negotiating are all that thousands of others have needed to be highly effective in these areas.

How to Turn Your Interviews Into Attractive Job Offers

Job hunting success depends 70% on marketing and interviewing and 30% on background and ability.

The first key to becoming great at interviewing is to know how to build personal chemistry.

Your starting point is to have an interviewing game plan

Some people think interviews are just conversations, and others believe they are just sessions during which they have to answer questions. These things may happen, but an interview that turns into an offer involves far more.

Think about this. Last year there were more than 200 million interviews, and no two were the same. So how do you prepare? You do it the same way you would for a sports contest. There were millions of them and none were the same.

In an interview or a sports contest, you can't plan precisely how things will go, but you can have a game plan. That means knowing the points you want to touch on and the pace you want to maintain.

Interviewing, of course, is a selling situation. It involves the exchange of information and the building of personal chemistry. Naturally, it's not only what you say that's important. Let's look now at the seven key things you can do to build a positive rapport.

1 Research can help build chemistry

This leads us to your first step for building chemistry, and it involves researching the company in advance. Did you ever meet anyone for the first time who knew a lot about you? It takes you by surprise, doesn't it? It's a great way to make a positive first impression.

Many people have built successful businesses that way. One friend of mine, a consultant with a six-figure income, attributes his entire success to the research he does ahead of time.

Four out of every five of his clients tell him that he wins their business because he knows a lot more about them than anyone else. So make it your business to know as much as you can about the company, the industry, and if possible, about the person you'll be meeting.

When you arrange or confirm an appointment, never allow yourself to come across as flat or lacking in personality. Be sure to use the opportunity to gather more information. Many people have been able to get job descriptions, organization charts and brochures ahead of time by simply requesting them over the phone. That will help prepare you to be able to build better chemistry in your interview.

2 Build chemistry with the front office staff

Can you guess what percentage of executives say their secretaries' opinions influence them? What do you think? One-third? Half? Well, about two-thirds of them do.

Here's how this might affect you. Not too long ago, I was interrupted by Hattie, who stated that Mr. Baxter had arrived for his 2:00 interview. I had forgotten about the appointment and it was a busy day. I immediately asked, "What do you think of him, Hattie?" She didn't say a word. She just gave a thumbs-down signal.

That was the end for poor Baxter. No one ever taught him how important it is to make a positive impression with the front office staff. I told Hattie to have him see one of my assistants and to tell him her opinion first.

So, please be attentive to the secretary and others who work up front. Remember, you can do more than make friends. Have a conversation that gives you information that will help in the interview. If you have to wait, and the secretary is too busy to talk, give the impression that you can put the waiting time to good use.

You may find, as many people have, that when you go out of your way to be respectful to them, they will often go out of their way to help you.

In some cases, a secretary even will go so far as to call you to let you know when the boss is finally there and available and in a good mood.

3 Build chemistry with your attitude and image

Psychologists tell us that the way we expect to be treated has a lot to do with the way we are treated. So build positive expectations and picture a friendly interviewer.

Of course, you have to realize that many employers reach a negative decision in the first five minutes of an interview.

Why? Well, if you have the credentials, you've either established a good initial impression or you haven't. And what determines this personal chemistry?

People silently react to the image you project, your posture and body language, the things you say about any subject at all, and the way you answer questions.

Consider the kind of image you project. After all, each of us is continually projecting some kind of image.

It isn't just physical image or dress either, although your appearance speaks before you say a word. It's also a matter of attitude, interest, enthusiasm and your outlook on life.

Check your image before you ever get to the interview, but don't be too kind to yourself. Go to someone who is not really close to you and ask them what kind of an attitude they think you project. Ask for their honest opinion of your appearance, eye contact and mannerisms.

Listen to what they have to say, then check out the same things with someone on your side. Somewhere between the two, there will be an accurate picture, and if anything needs to be worked on, do it.

4 Build chemistry by paying sincere compliments

Do people like receiving compliments? You bet they do. So, before the interview, read or talk to people about the company and uncover some good things to say. Somewhere in those first few minutes, find the opportunity to let the interviewer know that you heard good things.

This will accomplish the following. It will show that you know something about the company, and it's also what we call a "third-party compliment," where you are passing on the good news that you heard from others. Now, you can compliment their facilities, people, products, advertising, public relations or anything else. Whatever you do, be specific.

Don't just say that people you know are impressed by the product. Talk about why they are impressed. Maybe it's that new product they added this year, or the designs they've adapted. Or maybe it's the reliability of their products.

All of us like to hear about how our products have pleased customers. By giving details, you show that you have given it some thought and that your compliment is not just empty flattery.

5 Build chemistry in the way you answer questions

The way you answer questions has more to do with building positive chemistry than with what you say. For example, suppose you get the old standby, "Tell me about yourself." After all, 25% of all interviews include a form of that question.

You'll want to answer, but chances are you're not sure what they want to hear. You could start out by talking about the kind of person you are and some of your attributes, but that may not be what the interviewer is interested in.

Faced with such a dilemma, a safe way out is to self-qualify your answer. "Certainly, Mr. Jones, I'd be happy to tell you about myself, and I suppose you are most interested in my work experience. I'll focus on the past few years and how they relate to this position. I can start with my most recent experience and work backwards if you like."

When you self-qualify like that, you give the interviewer plenty of opportunity to respond, and to direct the conversation toward some other area, if that's not what he or she is really interested in. That way you can avoid talking for ten minutes about the wrong things.

Answer questions with good, action-oriented stories. If you fail to tell a story, do you think the interviewer will remember the conversation? Don't bet on it. People don't remember answers to questions or concepts. What people remember, and what impresses most of them are stories— good stories— action-oriented stories.

After-dinner speakers know this, famous coaches and motivators know it, preachers know it. Stories are the best way to make a point. So why not avoid the simple "yes" answer and have stories ready to make your best points. Use our SODAR technique as described in Chapter Two.

When you answer questions, remember to gear your comments to potential contributions relative to sales, profits, cost reduction, efficiency, innovations or whatever.

When there is a silence, have questions about the field for which you have answers. Create an opportunity to demonstrate your knowledge. Being prepared builds confidence. It also means being more spontaneous. At all times, keep eye contact and establish your sincerity and integrity.

When you encounter difficult questions, one way to handle them is with the "U-turn" technique. For example, let's say an interviewer says, "You look very impressive on paper, Chuck. If you're this good, you ought to be able to solve all of our problems. Tell me, why should we hire you?" Now, of course, you know the person doesn't believe you're that good.

However, if you begin to talk about why they should hire you, you run the real risk of going on at length about all the wrong things. With the "U-turn" technique you don't give an answer. Instead, you turn the question around in a way that acknowledges the status of the interviewer and maybe even pays an indirect compliment.

Your comment might go something like this. "I have a lot of experience I believe this firm could use. But it would be presumptuous of me to tell you what you need before I've even shown the courtesy of listening to what you think the priorities are.

If you'd be kind enough to share some of your thoughts on these priorities, perhaps I could give a more intelligent answer." With a response like that, you are very likely to get a knowing smile, often followed by a careful explanation of the way things really are in that company.

Here are some sample answers to questions you are likely to encounter

What is your weakness?

"Well, I really don't feel I have a weakness which affects my working ability. At times I have a tendency to be impatient and occasionally push people too hard to get a job done."

What do you think of your boss?

"He's outstanding. I have enjoyed working with him."

When could you make a contribution?

"Well, I hope to be able to make a contribution in a very short time. Obviously, it will take some time to get my feet wet. However, there are a number of things which I have accomplished before that I may be able to institute once I gain a better understanding of your organization."

How long would you stay with us?

"As I mentioned to you, I'm looking for a career. However, I'm a realist. If I don't do the job, you won't want me around, and if there is no opportunity, it won't be right for me."

What's wrong with your firm?

"I really don't feel there is anything wrong with the firm. I have enjoyed working there, and they have some really top people in management. It's a good company, but I am ready to handle additional responsibility right now."

Why are you leaving?

"I'm anxious to earn more money and take on added responsibility. I'd also like to expand my knowledge. Quite frankly, these opportunities don't exist in my present firm."

6 Listen, find out what they want and build chemistry as you do it

I said earlier that an interview is like a sales call, and the key to making any sale is finding out what the customer really wants. So, how do you find out what they want? Well, sometimes the interviewer will get directly to the point and tell you exactly what they are looking for. That makes it easy. All you need to do is take your listening ability and put it to work.

When you run into people who are not good interviewers, be ready to ask job-related questions that will start this person talking about the areas in which you can help the company.

Don't expect to be able to think of these questions suddenly in the interview, and be sure to keep them geared toward areas where you can help the company. One of the easiest ways to impress people is to ask intelligent and penetrating questions about the firm and the position.

Find out what happened to the last person in the job. Ask the interviewer about his interests and experiences and that of his superiors and the CEO. If a situation stalls, raise questions about any subject by simply asking who? what? when? where? why? and how?

Find out who the position reports to and how long they have been in the job. Pinpoint the authority that goes with the job, and find out what they expect you to accomplish in the first six months.

You could ask a simple question such as, "What would be the biggest challenge I would face?" If the interviewer has some reservations, ask a question that is likely to flush them out. Don't forget that you're better off knowing their concerns. That way you can deal with them.

Of most importance, find out how the interviewer sees the problem, what their expectations are and the progress that has been made. When you do this, you're learning what the unwritten requirements of the job are.

7 Let employers know you have what they want

Let's assume that you've asked the right kinds of questions and done enough listening. Now you know what they want. It's time for the third essential part of the interview. It's time to let them know you have what they want— and you need to build chemistry as you do it. To do this well calls for advance preparation. Ideally, at this stage you should have your own 2-minute interviewing commercial ready to go. Again, the purpose is to let them know you have what they want!

One of the best ways to do this is with SODAR stories. Those are the action-oriented stories referred to earlier and explained in Chapter Two.

After you've given your SODAR story, make sure you ask for feedback. You might ask, for instance, "Is that the kind of approach you think you might need here?" A positive response from the interviewer will help fix the story in his or her memory. Your conversations may follow a general pattern. First, ask a question. Second, engage in conversation so you can listen. Third, get across that you have the required strengths. Fourth, ask a feedback question.

Now it's time to determine if you want the job, and you need to keep your chemistry while you do it. So, before the conclusion of any interview, you need to get some specific feedback. One way to do this is to verbalize a positive summary of the meeting, pointing out your enthusiasm about the job.

After the summary, ask a question that will generate feedback: *"In your opinion, are my skills and strengths as closely matched to your needs as I think they are? How can we pursue our interests further?"*

Now that you have a game plan for building chemistry, I hope you will gain an extra sense of confidence from knowing what you intend to do and being very well prepared to do it.

The second key to becoming
great at interviewing, is
to handle whatever
objections may come up—
and to do it in a way that
is comfortable for you.

The "Iceberg" approach

Many of us are more conscious of our liabilities than our strengths. When confronted with a liability, we may become defensive, argumentative, or worst of all, acquiescent.

When dealing with sensitive issues, you want to remain atop the iceberg, well removed from the possibility of drowning! If challenged, relinquish as little information as possible— just small slices off the top. The key to making this approach work is projection: positive, non-defensive and non-evasive.

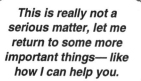

This is really not a serious matter, let me return to some more important things— like how I can help you.

For example, consider the case in which you had been terminated. The sequence might proceed as follows.

Employer: Are you unemployed?

You: (1st slice) Why, yes I am. I left ABC in June.

Employer: Why were you terminated?

You: (2nd slice) My position was eliminated in a corporate reorganization.

Employer: Why were you let go?

You: (3rd slice) In today's economy, good jobs in retrenchment situations are difficult to find. In my case, I was offered a position, but since I'd like to move forward, rather than laterally, I elected to seek a new challenge outside the firm.

Note that all the statements are brief, positive with no recriminations and responsive to the question asked.

The "ARTS" approach

As mentioned, when faced with objections, the tendency of many people is to become defensive. However, no one ever sells anything to people while they are arguing with them.

It is important to have a valid answer when an objection is raised, but jumping to the answer may seem defensive. To avoid that trap you can use a simple process called ARTS. It can frequently convert a liability into a perceived asset. The letters stand for the following.

"With the ARTS approach, you never need to feel that you're under attack."

A— Acknowledge the objection
R— Redirect the person's concern
T— Test to be sure you've removed their concern
S— Use a story to make your point

Now let's look at how you can make this work.

A = Acknowledge the objection

"I thought you might be concerned about that... and frankly, if I were in your position, I'd be asking the same question."

Whenever someone raises an objection, the tension level rises. What you want to achieve in step one is to reduce the tension level. Here's how it might work. "I can understand your concern. It is certainly something we should discuss, and I would like to address it directly for you." Or..."You're very perceptive and you've raised an interesting point. It deserves some frank discussion, and I'd like to address it for you."

The phrases you might use are not so important. Instead, it's the feeling you impart. You haven't gotten flustered. You have acted in a friendly and reassuring way, and that implies you feel secure about your abilities in the area under question.

R = Redirect the conversation

"What positive qualities are you looking for in the ideal candidate that prompted you to bring this up?"

Let's say the interviewer raised the objection that your experience was in a different industry.

Now, you can't do too much about the fact that your experience was in a different industry, but you probably can show that you are someone who contributes quickly, so that is where you want to direct the conversation.

For example, "When you raise that question, I understand that you want to be sure the person you put in this job is someone who will contribute quickly. Isn't that it?" This gives the interviewer the opportunity to positively reaffirm that you are indeed correct.

Also, in case you did misinterpret, it will give the interviewer the chance to tell you so. In the unlikely event that this were to happen, you could always say something such as, "Oh, I must have made the wrong assumption. Tell me, what kind of positive qualities are you looking for that prompted you to bring this up?"

With just a little thought, it is very easy to refocus the conversation toward the positive qualities that are really on the interviewer's mind.

T = Ask a testing question

*"If I could show that I could contribute quickly... even
when it comes to learning a great deal of
new information... would that help?"*

After you get a positive response, you have the option of going
directly to your answer, or you can introduce one of your key
strengths. You might say: "If I could show you that I work well
under pressure, might that ease your concern somewhat?" If
possible, use a supporting story as part of your answer, ending
it with a feedback question that will keep the conversation on
the positive side.

S = Tell a story to answer the objection

*"I'd like to tell you a story that relates
very closely to your problem."*

Remember, what really counts is the fact that you did not get
flustered. Instead, you had a friendly exchange in which you
built positive feelings. If you've done it right, interviewers
won't be all that concerned about whether your answer is
exactly correct. Instead, they'll be thinking, "This person
handled that situation very well." Learn how to use this
process, and for every concern, you should, of course, have
your answer ready.

Be ready for application forms and tests

Always type or print neatly. Never fill them out in a hurry, and try to do them at home.

❑

Delay giving references until interest exists. If a salary objective is requested on a given form, leave it blank. It is impossible to guess exactly how much a position is worth and stating your objective will only limit your ability to negotiate.

❑

When you complete your career history, expand on the accomplishments and duties section by referring to your resume.

❑

Reflect an active personality. Mention hobbies, sports, civic and social interests, etc.

❑

Questions along the line of, "Have you been arrested or denied credit?" invite a careful response. If you have a problem, it is illegal for an employer to ask these questions under the Equal Employment Opportunity Law.

❑

When you return your application, attach a cover letter which clearly restates your interest with enthusiasm.

❑

In the 90s testing is more in vogue than ever before. Be sure to approach them with care. Widely used tests have fallen into the hands of many people who are skilled at taking tests.

Common situations
to avoid

Try to avoid arriving more than 7 minutes early. If you are kept waiting too long, then ask for another appointment and excuse yourself. Also, don't bring packages with you.

❏

At lunch don't select sloppy or hard-to-manage foods. Take your cue on drinks from the interviewer. Avoid smoking and be careful about posing a threat to anyone's philosophical position.

❏

Never read mail on your interviewer's desk, drum your fingers, look at your watch, or exhibit other signs of boredom.

❏

Avoid discussions on race, religion or politics. Don't be a "yes-man," don't interrupt, don't lose your temper and don't be a braggart. Also, don't criticize your past employers; don't name-drop unless you can be very smooth about it; and never apologize for liabilities.

❏

Don't let an interview carry on too long. When a discussion peaks, diplomatically lead to an end of the meeting. Also, don't linger after the interview.

❏

It's a bad sign if an interviewer accepts phone calls, but a good sign if the interviewer does more talking than you do, or if he begins to talk about your solving his problem.

❏

There will always be some questions for which you can't have answers. Don't let this bother you. After a while you will find that even difficult situations will leave you relatively un-ruffled.

Commonly asked interview questions

Employment / Management Style

- ❏ Why did you join your present firm?
- ❏ Why are you leaving?
- ❏ How would you evaluate your present firm?
- ❏ Have you managed people before?
- ❏ What are your capabilities that will help us?
- ❏ What major challenges have you faced?
- ❏ Have you fired people before?
- ❏ What references can you give me?
- ❏ Does your employer know you are looking?
- ❏ Why have you stayed so long?
- ❏ Describe a typical day in your job.
- ❏ What areas of your job do you enjoy?
- ❏ How do you feel about your previous moves?
- ❏ Which firms did you enjoy the most?
- ❏ What parts of your job do you enjoy the most?
- ❏ How well do you handle pressure?
- ❏ What do you look for when you hire people?
- ❏ What do you think of your ex-boss?
- ❏ Why haven't you found a job so far?
- ❏ How does the firm view your performance?
- ❏ Which areas of your performance have been criticized?
- ❏ Is there anything that might hinder your ability to perform with our company?

- ❏ Can you work independently?
- ❏ Can you fit in an unstructured environment?
- ❏ How have you helped reduce costs?
- ❏ What was your greatest accomplishment in your present or last job?
- ❏ Describe your management style.
- ❏ How effective are you as a motivator?
- ❏ What decisions do you delegate?
- ❏ What types of controls do you use?
- ❏ What are your strengths? Weaknesses?
- ❏ Would you classify yourself as a leader?
- ❏ How hard do you work?
- ❏ How do you handle confrontation?

Education / Compensation

- ❏ What full- or part-time jobs did you hold while in school?
- ❏ What subjects did you enjoy most? Least?
- ❏ How were your college grades and class rank?
- ❏ What about other activities?
- ❏ What specialized training have you received?
- ❏ Why didn't you do better in school?
- ❏ How did you finance your education?
- ❏ How have your education and training prepared you for this job?
- ❏ What is your current compensation?
- ❏ How often have you had raises?
- ❏ What do you think you are worth?

- Why does your compensation seem so low?
- What would like to be earning 2 / 4 years from now?
- What were your highest earnings?

Character Traits /Personal

- What are the reasons for your success?
- Who are your closest friends? What do they do?
- How often have you been absent from work?
- How often do you lose your temper?
- How confident are you about addressing a group?
- How would a friend describe you?
- Would you work if you did not need money?
- What do you do when you have trouble solving a problem?
- Have you ever been arrested or convicted?
- What are your hobbies?
- How do you spend your spare time?
- Are you active in your community?
- When was your last vacation?
- Are you interested in sports?
- What part of the newspaper do you turn to first?
- What was the last book you read?
- Have you ever been refused a bond?
- How much debt do you have?

- Have you ever gone bankrupt?
- In what areas can you improve?

Miscellaneous

- Tell me about yourself.
- How old are you?
- What is your political party affiliation?
- Would you object to working for a woman?
- What is your present financial situation?
- Who do you admire?
- Why did your business fail?
- How are your writing skills?
- What work environment are you looking for?
- If you had your choice of jobs and companies where would you go?
- Why are you interested in our position?
- How long can we expect you to stay with us?
- Why should we hire you?
- Where else are you interviewing and what other offers have you received?

Image building for men...
looking good and feeling confident

Your third key to interviewing success is to always be ready to project the right image. This summary is only intended as a brief guideline. However, if you have time, there are numerous books on the subject of dress which are worthwhile reading.

Overall impressions are established within the first few minutes of a meeting. So, before you launch your campaign, assess your wardrobe. You should have a few appropriate "classic" outfits because you must expect to go through a series of interviews. Avoid wearing the same attire twice.

You must realize that interviewers may be talking to four or five other candidates. Use your clothing to project a personality that fits the situation and the firm. As a general rule, when it comes to interviewing, a "straight-arrow" look works.

For interviewing, most people will do best if their suits are properly fitted and conservative. A balanced job search wardrobe will ideally include a navy blue suit, a darker gray and a charcoal pin-stripe. High fashion and extreme styles are not suitable unless you are in one of the "glamour" industries.

One of the most difficult things for most men to do is throw away suits. If your suits are old, give them to charity and take the tax deduction.

Wallet, credit cards and other paraphernalia should be kept in a briefcase. This latter practice is more common among top executives. By the way, allow 5" from the top of your thumb to the end of your sleeve— 5 1/4" if you wear cuff links. Don't let tailors persuade you to take longer sleeves!

Clothing must fit properly. This is particularly true with suits, which sometimes slowly shrink with dry cleaning. Be prepared to go back a number of times for alterations, and make sure your pants cuff barely touches your shoe.

As for your shirts, solid colors are recommended, with white and blue being traditional and safe preferences. Wear these colors in the interviews, or until you have the opportunity to assess the working environment you are exploring.

The fit of your shirt deserves special mention. If you have gained a significant amount of weight, you may be wearing your collar too tight.

Ex-athletes who have trimmed down will often find that their collars have become loose. A well-fitting collar makes a tie a pleasure to wear for the entire business day. The fit of your cuffs is also important.

The most popular shirt over the years has been the 100% cotton long-sleeved, pointed-collar business shirt. Generally speaking, you will want to avoid short-sleeved shirts unless you live in a warm climate. A word of caution: Be sure that the front and collar are not rippled. This will give you a "sloppy" image. Those who wear cuff links should make sure they are simple. A gaudy look is likely to be perceived as a negative.

Why not buy a few ties for your job search? Ties can be fun and can give you a unique look. To a great extent, this element of your wardrobe is a matter of preference. For most people silk ties are best. Be sure you don't select a tie that is too flimsy. It should have adequate backing for you to look your best.

Pattern, polka-dot, and club ties have declined in popularity. The brighter, more contemporary geometric and floral designs also come in a wide array of vivid color combinations that are in good taste. Above all, be sure your tie is clean and fresh in appearance. Bow ties will do little to enhance your image of assurance.

Your shoes should be well polished. Slip-ons are increasingly acceptable but eyelet shoes are still preferred. The old military "spitshine" can be a real power builder.

Don't underrate accessories. Don't wear your deep sea watch, unless it's a Rolex. Ideally, your watch will be light or medium in weight. Belts and buckles should be conservative. Socks should be over the calf in length. It is not necessary to have a handkerchief tucked in your breast pocket, but it can be a nice touch. The handkerchief you carry should be clean and pressed. A wallet and briefcase show a lot about a man. *Bulging wallets and oversize briefcases can detract.*

Your hair style should be natural and causal. As a rule, if you appear older than you would like, your hair should be on the short side. *(Short hair will normally give you a younger appearance.)* For most men in their 20s or 30s, however, a somewhat longer look is appropriate.

Be sure your glasses are clean and in good condition. For late afternoon interviews, carry an electric razor in your briefcase and shave an hour or two before. Be sure to have your barber trim facial hairs (including nose and ears) before your meeting. As far as after-shave or cologne is concerned, keep it subtle or don't use it at all.

For those of you who are overweight, clothes can cover up just so much. Lose some extra pounds if at all possible. If not, stand up straight, sit tall and be yourself. Carry yourself in a way that creates a look of confidence and authority. Remember, when you are job hunting, the people you meet socially can be instrumental in helping you land an attractive new position.

Image building for women... looking good and feeling confident

Elegant, self-assured, knowledgeable— what woman wouldn't want to convey these qualities to an employer? However, to make the best possible impression, make some preparation.

A woman who "looks right" for the job makes it easier for any potential employer to make a positive decision. By creating the best possible appearance, you also enhance your self-confidence. You want to feel great about yourself.

Clothes tell the employer how you see yourself. Your hairstyle and your choice of makeup is either going to reinforce or detract from your professional image. The accessories you choose— shoes, purse, jewelry, etc., make a further statement about your awareness of that image.

There is no single look for all women. The suit, as the "uniform" for a woman aspiring to a managerial position, is no longer an absolute rule. Guidelines about dress have become more flexible. "Presence" involves not only appearance but also self-confidence and knowledge.

A good haircut is essential. Short to medium-length hair is most appropriate for the woman seeking a professional position. Keep away from an "extreme" look. Your makeup should appear natural. If you're not sure whether your present makeup is appropriate, try out some advice at the cosmetics counter of a good department store.

Whatever you do, make any changes well in advance of your interview. It is important that you feel comfortable with any "new look" so you won't be anxious on the day of the interview. Your nails should be medium length. Keep away from shades that are distracting. If you are accustomed to wearing fragrance, make sure it isn't heavy. Never wear anything that is overpowering. While a beautifully tailored suit is always appropriate, you can arrive for an interview in a co-ordinating jacket and skirt (complemented by a minimum of jewelry) and carrying a light briefcase; this would be a very acceptable look.

When choosing colors, keep to an understated, conservative look. A solid color, a muted tweed or plaid, or a subtle pinstripe is always in good taste. You want your next employer to remember *you,* not your outfit.

If you generally wear bright colors, you can retain your personal style by choosing a scarf or blouse in a shade you particularly enjoy. The blouse or sweater you select to go with your suit should either be white, off-white, beige or a color complementary to your suit. For example, a scarlet or crimson blouse can brighten up a grey suit and contribute to your appearance, especially if red is a color you enjoy wearing.

Generally, your stockings should be neutral. Stay away from heavily textured or patterned stockings. As for shoes, keep away from extreme high heels, sandals and flat shoes.

Keep your jewelry simple. Wearing four rings won't help you here! The key is never use anything so startling or overbearing that it detracts from the overall impression you want to make. The key point to remember is that good dress won't get you a job— but sloppy dress can cost you one. Be aware that there is an unspoken "managerial" dress code for women. It is more tailored than feminine (no plunging necklines or sheer fabrics) and enhances a "power" look.

These emphasize a woman's ability to perform on the job, rather than her femininity. Make sure you look like you are ready for the income level to which you aspire. Body language is also important. Straight posture says that you take pride in your appearance. Graceful hand movements contribute to your overall image of poise.

How to Negotiate Your Best Financial Offer

The following negotiation process is easy to use. It's about common sense and the art of soft selling. It works!

In negotiating a job offer— winning is not everything

There have been many books written by people who call themselves experts in negotiations, but they emphasize situations where you negotiate with someone you will never deal with again. Their philosophy is that winning is everything.

However, in the job search situation, the use of intimidation and attack strategies have no value. Techniques for one-upmanship can cost you the job. Here you're setting the tone for your long-term relationship.

Never allow yourself to be seen as overly aggressive. In fact, the reason most people don't like the term "negotiation" is that they associate it with confrontation, being tough and role playing something that does not come naturally.

The truth is the best negotiators are low-key. They avoid anything that might cause irritations. So remember, never project an image of being argumentative or emotional. Follow the best negotiators and make sure you appear sincere and reasonable— never cold or calculating.

1 Start negotiating only after the employer is sold on you

Never attempt to negotiate until the employer is sold on you. Many people misunderstand and think of negotiation as selling. In truth, you cannot negotiate unless there is some hope that you can get the employer to offer new terms, and there is almost no chance they would offer you new terms unless they were sold on you.

When you are ready to negotiate, you will find it helpful to have clear ideas about what you want. Realizing that you will not achieve everything, keep your main objectives in mind, and do not risk an entire negotiation by coming on too strong about less important points.

Support what you want with only one or two strong reasons, rather than many which may be strong or weak. The moment you give a weak reason, the employer can use that as an excuse for not granting the item in question.

2 Never be afraid to ask for what you want

No one will ever withdraw an offer because you ask for something in addition. You should always sell "quality" rather than "low starting price." After all, the easier you are to get, the less you'll be valued when you come aboard. If you are looking to change for a financial reason, don't appear greedy, but looking for a 15% to 33% increase is acceptable.

This is significant because people at salaries from $25,000 through $300,000 have won increases of 25%, 50% and even 100%. This is not to say it is easy, but don't lower your goals without first testing your marketability.

You need to understand compensation systems. The salary for most jobs is usually flexible within a range that is set in advance. At the very least, an employer always has an idea of what he is willing to pay for an assignment.

One exception to this situation would be when an employer wants to hire you and is willing to create a new position to bring you aboard. That's always your best opportunity for negotiating something most attractive!

As a rule you should also focus on negotiating a percent increase. For example, subject to how much you are currently earning it is usually better to speak in terms of "percentages" instead of "thousands of dollars." It sounds like less.

3 Express some vulnerability to gain sympathy

Expressing a slight amount of vulnerability can be a very effective weapon in your negotiation process. It is done simply by letting the employer know that accepting the job on the terms offered would cause you some personal difficulties.

This plays to the employer's desire to make sure you are happy, so you can devote your full energies to the job.

For example, you can be flattered by the offer, but you can say that you may have to sacrifice your current life-style in order to afford to take the job. And, of course, this would disappoint your family.

"I love the job and really want to join with you, but we'd have difficulty making ends meet. Is there a chance you could go a little higher?"

4 Question— rather than demand

The best negotiators persuade others through questions. This gives them the information they need to put themselves in control of the situation. It also gives them time to think and never has them putting all their cards on the table.

For instance, good negotiators will not say, "I do not agree with you because..." Rather, they will say, *"Frank, you do make a good point, but I wonder if there is room for another point of view..."* or *"I accept that point of view, but it raises a question about..."*

They would never say, *"That would not be any good for me."* Instead, they might say, *"Bill, could you tell me how you think this would work for me?"*

Then, they will follow up with questions, so the employer can discover for himself that the proposal is not quite good enough. And that is your goal: to let the company discover for themselves the validity of your request.

They might never be persuaded if you tell them their point of view is wrong, but if your questions lead them to discover it, they will be much more disposed to changing the terms. So remember, question— do not demand.

5 Negotiate the nature of the job and the responsibilities

This is the most important factor you need to negotiate. The reason you need to do this is because the range in which you will negotiate compensation is determined by the responsibilities that go with the job. If you can reshape the job into a larger one, the salary range will be higher.

How much responsibility can I negotiate... Sales Rep? Manager? or VP?

To get started, begin with a positive comment about the job and the firm; suggest that they might benefit by adding responsibilities to the job. Then offer to share your thoughts on what might be added.

For example, *"Tom, there is no doubt that this is a good job. However, based on what you have told me, I believe I could be even more helpful if a few related elements were added. There are three areas where my experience could make a big difference. I'd like to discuss them, so we could see whether they could be included in the job description."*

You could then go on to talk about the areas where the firm could capitalize on your experience, showing with personal stories how you have made contributions before. If the interviewer agrees these are important, have them added to the job description. Believe it or not, reshaping the job can often be just that simple! Can you see how we have applied some of the basic principles here? There was no confrontation. The manner was positive, friendly and matter-of-fact.

6 Avoid discussing money until the time is right

Premature discussions about money or benefits can be a real deal breaker. Besides, the more enthusiastic an employer becomes about you— the more likely he'll be willing to pay more. So learn how to avoid premature discussion of money.

Sometimes an interviewer will begin with a statement like this: "Jim, before we get started, I need to know how much money you are looking for. I don't want to waste our time if it is totally out of the ball park." The principle to keep in mind here is that you do not have to answer the question! For example,

"Bill, frankly, I could talk more intelligently about my circumstances after I know a bit more about the job responsibilities and the growth that's possible in this position. Speaking of that, I noticed that you listed technical experience as one of the requirements for the job. Will this job have line manufacturing responsibilities?"

Or... "Bill, I appreciate your being direct. I would not take your time if I did not have a fairly good idea of the range you would be willing to pay. If we can agree that my experience fits your needs, I doubt we will have a problem on compensation.

Frankly, my concern is the basic question of whether your needs call for someone with my background. Incidentally, I've heard that you're entering a number of added markets with your new product. Is that where this job fits in?"

It is important to have your thoughts ready and use words you feel comfortable with. Before the interview, figure out how you would handle the situation in your own words. That way, your response will come quite naturally. Once again, our U-turn can help you here. It is a way to pleasantly avoid being the first to mention a figure. See the example on the next page.

Here's an example of the U-turn technique:

"For my part, I am most interested in finding a good situation in terms of challenge, growth possibilities and the people I am working with. So far, it seems that this position has it all. The company's commitment, the people and my role in the overall effort all have great appeal.

And while money is important, I'm not locked into a specific figure because these other considerations are important. Now that you have brought the subject up, though, what kind of range did you have in mind?"

Using this approach, you remain gracious and friendly while avoiding a direct answer. You will often find that the employer replies by giving you a stated range. If an interviewer persists about how much you earned or want to earn, you have to exercise judgment. Here is one possible response.

"I would rather avoid discussing my compensation until later on. Job content and challenge are most important to me, and I would like to talk money after I know you want me for the job. Is that agreeable to you?"

If all else fails, give a range which surrounds your best estimate of the upper end of what the job might pay.

7 When an offer is made, never say "yes" or "no" immediately

If you are offered a job, but the salary is too low, let the employer know how pleased you are they made an offer. Take the opportunity to praise the company and explain that you need some time to consider it. You might try a statement like this:

"John, I am pleased you made me an offer. This is an outstanding company and the position has a lot of promise. I am sure you can appreciate that I would like some time to give it further consideration. It would not present any problem, would it, if I were to get back to you tomorrow?"

When you call back, after opening with one or two positive statements, consider raising the possibility of redefining the job. Your conversation might be something like this:

"John, I appreciate the fact that you gave me the time to consider the job further. As I said earlier, the idea of joining your firm is exciting, and the position is very appealing in many respects. I want the job, but I have difficulty with the level of starting salary."

"With children about to enter college, I had done some planning based on an income that was $5,000 higher. As I thought about that, however, I realized that jobs are not cast in bronze and that a company can often redefine a position to fit the talents of the person they want. Would it be possible to take another look at the job specs?"

For my part, I know that if you could make a modest additional investment, I would show you a handsome return through my performance. I sincerely want to work for you and hope that we can make some adjustment. Can we take a look at it?"

Of course there may be situations where you do not want to redefine the job, but you would still like to raise the salary. In that case you use the same technique, but show some vulnerability, then suggest that a specific dollar figure be added to the base salary.

Normally, if that figure is within 10% to 15% of what you have been offered, the employer will not take offense and will grant you at least a part of it.

Once again, the reason for the positive statement is to reassure the employer that you think the offer is fair. Asking for more money is a negative, and it needs to be balanced by positives. If your positive comments are too brief, the employer would only hear the negative, the request for more money. Here is an approach that you might consider.

> " *John, I cannot tell you how pleased I am to receive this offer. The challenge is obviously there, and I think my experience is perfect for the job. What I am most enthusiastic about is that I felt such a positive chemistry with everyone I met. There is one problem, however. You see, one of the main reasons I wanted to make a change was for financial balance. Can you see your way clear to adding $5,000 to the base? It would ease my family situation a lot.* "

8 Use your enthusiasm as a major negotiating technique

If you load a maximum amount of enthusiasm into your statements, it becomes nearly impossible for the employer to conclude that you should not be with them.

Enthusiasm can be particularly important when you have been underpaid. Ideally, an offer should be based on your value to the company, but in reality, most employers will base their offers on present earnings.

When you get back to them, however, follow the principle of introducing other criteria on which to base the offer. This can include the importance of the job to the company, what you would make with a raise where you are, your total compensation package, what you believe the market is for persons with your background, or any other offers you are considering.

In the example that follows, notice how there are no demands, only questions. By your inviting employers to explore the situation with you, they are free to reach their own conclusions about whether their offer is too low.

Using this approach, you come across as easy-going, sincere and slightly vulnerable, never as cold, calculating or aggressively demanding— never as someone who is putting them in a corner.

Your comment might be:

"Paul, let me first tell you once again how pleased I am that you made me an offer. I am very positive about the prospect of joining you.

I must never come across as aggressively demanding! I must come across as easy-going, sincere and slightly vulnerable.

I've had the chance now to give it some more thought, and I can only say that my enthusiasm has continued to increase. If we can forget about money for the moment, this is the job I want. It's the kind of situation where a person could look forward to staying with an exciting company for the long term.

There is one hurdle that I have to overcome. You see, I've been underpaid now for some time, and it has created a financial situation where I need to start earning at a rate which reflects my background and ability to contribute.

If I stayed where I am, I'd be due for a raise which would put me close to your offer. But it's because I know I am worth more than that, that I want to make a move.

In talking with other companies, I've discovered that some of them realize this, and they have mentioned ranges that are 25% higher. Now, I don't want to work for those companies. I want to work for you. But I do have some financial needs that just won't go away.

Is there some way we can get around this problem? Perhaps the company could approve a higher offer if they understood just how well qualified I am and how much I want to join the company. Can we pursue this together?"

Let's review all the things you might be able negotiate

In recent years firms have been more open to employment contracts. In the past contracts have usually guaranteed employees' compensation for a certain length of time, as long as people worked "to the best of their ability in normal business hours."

Under the terms of most contracts, employers are guaranteed very little, and the individual can usually break a contract quite easily. On the other hand, corporations are often forced into a settlement if they dismiss an executive under a contract, and the courts tend to favor individuals in these matters.

Today, a contract is just one more element in your total negotiation package. It may be just as negotiable as questions relating to salary, bonuses and stock option participation. If you can possibly arrange a contract, keep the following points in mind.

Keep the contract simple and try to keep your lawyer behind the scenes— out of the communication process. Try to make sure the following are incorporated into the contract: the length of the agreement, your specific assignment, your title, location, who you report to, your compensation, and what happens if there is a merger or if you are fired.

Some contracts can also cover bonus arrangements, deferred compensation, insurance, release with compensation in case of merger, salary benefits to your family in case of death, special reimbursement for foreign service, and outplacement in the event of termination.

From a company standpoint, you should expect that they will want you to enter a non-disclosure or trade secrecy agreement. This is a legitimate request.

If you are above $60,000, always bring up the subject of a contract. A request, as opposed to a demand, will never result in a revoked job offer. In most large companies, both signing bonuses and severance packages are spreading down the ladder. This is especially true when relocation is involved.

Obviously, there are certain firms with which you must be very firm about a contract. These would include companies in financial trouble, acquisition candidates, or those which have just been merged or been acquired, family-controlled organizations, and companies where one individual dominates the environment.

In any case don't ever make the mistake of treating contract terms lightly, and be sure to review all the fine print with a lawyer.

If you can't get a formal contract—try for a termination agreement. These are often substitutes for employment contracts. They are usually in the form of a short letter in which an employer agrees to irrevocable severance.

Many people favor the idea of these agreements. While few companies will acknowledge it, in some industries these agreements have already become quite common for salary levels above $80,000. However, there are many instances when people earning $60,000 have been successful in negotiating termination agreements.

In most cases such agreements provide for a minimum severance compensation of six months' salary, relocation expenses, insurance for twelve months, and professional outplacement. Any agreement that you accept should cover all non-legal situations under which an employer may choose to terminate your services.

Try to negotiate for the future

If you don't have any success in your negotiations, then you should shift from the "present" and focus instead on "futures," e.g., a review after six months, a better title, an automatic increase after twelve months, etc. These are easier things for an employer to give.

With inflation always a threat, the whole area of salary negotiations has become more fluid. Guidelines have been set aside by employers in order to attract good candidates.

Still, many people allow themselves to be deceived by discussions focusing on before-tax annual dollars. From a financial standpoint, what you must be concerned with are the opportunities for improving your standard of living.

Before accepting an offer, you should calculate just what an increase means in terms of "added funds on a weekly or monthly basis." This generally puts things into a much more meaningful perspective.

If you are an executive, very little in the way of "rules of thumb" can be provided. However, it does help to take the time to write the positives and negatives on paper. While it is convenient if the highest offer is also the most attractive opportunity, things rarely work out that way.

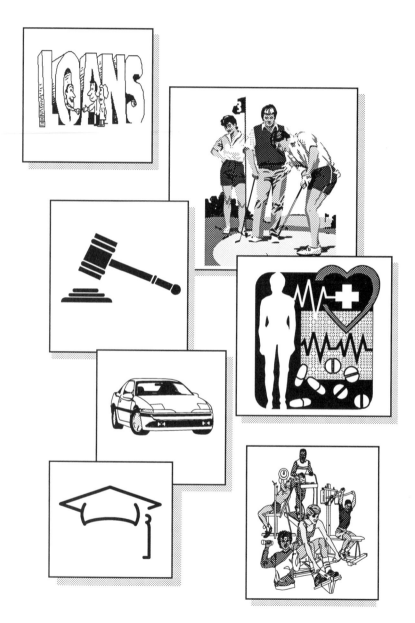

Other items that may be negotiable

Depending upon your situation, you may be able to negotiate many other forms of compensation. What follows is a brief discussion of major subjects which you might bring up during the course of your negotiations. Keep in mind that many perks may be out of reach because company policy excludes them for all.

Basics

- ❏ **Base salary and commissions.** Make sure that you fully understand any commission structure, and when and on what basis it is paid out.

- ❏ **Bonus.** The object for most people will be to negotiate a bonus related to their accomplishments. However, if you are a superstar, you might try for a signing bonus. Mid-level people can also get signing bonuses if relocation or partial loss of pension is involved.

- ❏ **Profit sharing pension plans.** Your next employer may have a program. Tax laws now mandate vesting rights at 5 to 7 years maximum. If you are negotiating a share of profits on a private basis, you need to understand the accounting methods of the company to insure the integrity of any understanding.

- ❏ **Medical and life insurance, dental and vision coverage.**

- ❏ **Severance payments.** For senior executives a standard agreement will cover two years, compensation. This should apply if you lose your job for any cause other than an illegal action. It should also be triggered if the company lessens your responsibilities or relocates you. Some severance payments have included private school tuition for dependents if you are relocated.

Stock options

❏ **Stock options purchase plans.** The company may allow you to purchase stock at market price and have them buy an equal amount under your name up to a percentage of your income (e.g., 6% of annual income).

❏ **Stock grants.** You may be able to negotiate stock as a gift. However, you will most likely be obligated to pay taxes based upon the market value of shares you are given.

❏ **ISOs (incentive stock options).** Some companies have arrangements which allow you to be granted the option to purchase a certain number of shares at market values of a given day. Generally, they won't allow you to exercise the option to buy them for a couple of years. The primary value of ISOs is that should you eventually buy them, no tax is due on the day you purchase the shares.

❏ **Restricted stock units.** Some firms will offer you an opportunity to receive stock units. They may peg the value of these units, for example, as one share of stock for every five units. The key question is when you can convert them to cash or shares.

❏ **Phantom stock options and stock appreciation rights.** Here you negotiate the right to receive the difference in market value between your shares at the time you are granted these rights and their value at the subsequent time when you can convert the rights to shares or cash.

❏ **Non-qualified stock options.** This is when a firm gives you an option to purchase stock below market prices. Whenever you exercise your options, tax will be due on the difference between the price at which you exercise your right of purchase and the market value of the stock.

Relocation expense and other perks

This includes company purchase of your home; moving expense; mortgage rate differential and pre-payment penalty; real estate brokerage; closing costs; cost of bridge loan; trips for family to look for a home; lodging fees between homes; tuition; installation of appliances, drapes and carpets; spouse outplacement assistance. Other executive perks can include:

❏ **Automobile**
❏ **Country club membership**
❏ **Child care**
❏ **Annual physical exam**
❏ **Luncheon club membership**
❏ **Athletic club membership**
❏ **Disability pay**
❏ **Legal assistance**
❏ **Consumer product discounts**
❏ **Executive dining room privileges**
❏ **Financial planning assistance**
❏ **Tuition reimbursement**
❏ **CPA and tax assistance**
❏ **Availability of short-term loans**
❏ **Insurance benefits after termination**
❏ **Outplacement assistance**
❏ **Deferred compensation**

It is most important that you first reach clear goals as to what you really want to negotiate. If you use our process for negotiating, you stand little chance of losing anything. No one is going to withdraw an offer just because you thought you were worth more. Once negotiations are completed, always confirm your understanding with a short letter.

Section Five:
Getting Into Action

This next section of this System will help you get into action in a timely manner, one that will enhance your chances for rapid success. It's just a very short chapter. However, the importance of organizing for your search is something that most people underestimate.

How to Organize and Launch Your Job Search

Being organized is your key to feeling good about your campaign and never becoming overwhelmed.
So use the checklist on the pages that follow to help yourself get into action.

Here's a checklist
to help you get into action

Your marketability and your career options

❑ Broaden your appeal by listing your experience according to the following: (a) business functions, (b) your skills and duties; and (c) your achievements.

❑ Inventory your areas of knowledge and interests.

❑ Since the opportunity you represent can be marketable, list the problems you can help an employer solve.

❑ Remember that your personality, enthusiasm and character may also be marketable.

❑ Decide how to handle your liabilities. See Chapter 15.

❑ Start searching out career and industry options.

Job hunting techniques

❑ Flip through each page of this system so that you are set on all of your job hunting strategies and techniques.

Your communications plan

❑ Develop a communications plan and SODAR stories.

❑ Prepare answers for overcoming possible objections; and answers for likely questions. Review Chapter 12.

❑ Develop your 30 second telephone commercial and your 2-minute interview commercial

❑ Prepare in advance for negotiations. Review Chapter 13.

Your resumes & letters

❑ Select a resume format and sketch a layout that will work for you. Prepare drafts of your resumes see Chapter 11.

❑ Take the key elements of your narrative resumes and adapt them for the copy points in your letters.

Your personal action plan

❑ Establish your action plan for getting interviews and prepare your references. See Chapters 3 through 9.

Researching organizations to contact

❑ Prepare your priority list of prospects.

*Prime prospects— best of best
*Prime prospects— others
*Secondary prospects
*Recruiters to contact

Other research

❑ Clip all possible job ads from the last 13 weeks.

❑ Begin your daily search for spot opportunities.

❑ Develop the broadest possible list of your potential networking contacts. Be willing to go back to people from years ago or to even remote possibilities.

❑ Plan your networking efforts. See Chapter 7.

Administrative

❑ Order your stationery and print your resume(s).

❑ Subscribe to appropriate newspapers.

❑ Make arrangements for office space, word processing, and any other office or telephone answering support you might require.

❑ If you require secrecy, make third-party arrangements.

❑ Keep careful records of all job search expenses. Current tax laws allow job hunting expenses such as deductions in all situations other than extreme career changes.

Implementation of your campaign

As mentioned earlier, no one will need to take all of our recommended actions. However, the more that you do, the greater your chances for timely success.

1   Answer old ads from the previous 13 weeks.

2   Launch your large macro marketing effort to the employers on your priority list.

3   Set aside time to follow up via telephone on selected correspondence as mentioned above.

4   Launch your mailing to recruiters.

5   Start networking personal acquaintances when you are sure your goals and materials are unlikely to change.

6   Network influentials and those related to industries you would consider.

7   Read the local and national business press daily for spot opportunities, and act on them as soon as possible.

8   Launch your custom micro marketing campaign to your best prospects on your priority list. Seven days later do your telephone follow-up.

On an ongoing basis

9   Answer ads using upgrading, downgrading and sidegrading techniques to increase your possibilities.

10   Respond to spot opportunities.

11   Make networking a continuous effort as you initiate the widest variety of possible actions. Contact new recruiters as you learn of them.

12   Add to your priority list as you learn of new organizations of interest. Adjust your plan and recycle your activity on the same action steps. Be resourceful, persistent, keep your attitude positive and work every day.

What to do if your actions fail to produce

Among the people who really implement this system, only a small percentage will encounter serious problems. If you find that it is not producing what you need, then consider the following actions.

If you are not getting enough interviews:

First, take a look at the scope of your effort. Are you getting enough copies of your credentials into the hands of the right people? Remember, job hunting is a numbers game. All other things being equal, the greater the number of contacts you make, the more opportunities you will have to explore.

No one needs to use all of the avenues presented as part of this system, but have you excluded some that you should be using? How much time are you really devoting to your search? Is the time committed in line with the importance you attach to making the right move at this stage of your career?

In addition, consider whether you are taking sufficient follow-through actions. Are you taking advantage of our phone techniques to telemarket yourself, and are you following up?

Second, if you are on target concerning the above, make a careful review of the materials you have been using. Writing resumes and letters is no different from any other form of creative writing. After intensely working on projects, professional writers need to put their work down for brief periods.

After you have stepped back, the words and phrases in your materials may look different. See if you think your story still gives convincing support to your objective. Perhaps some adjustments are in order? My experience has been that a fresh approach to your presentation can often make the entire difference.

Third, review your objectives. Are you sure your goals are clear? Is there a market for the kind of work you would like to do? Perhaps you need to consider widening your objectives either horizontally or vertically? Having been into your search for a while, can you identify any different options that might be appropriate?

Fourth, consider recycling your campaign along the lines of the same implementation phases as outlined two pages back. All of your main action avenues are there, so make some appropriate adjustments in your action plan.

If you are getting interviews, but not converting them into attractive offers:

First, if you have not been in the job market for a while, both your interviewing presentation and your interviewing skills may be a bit rusty. Go back and review the chapter on interviewing. Is there anything you are skipping in the process for building personal chemistry?

Second, review our system for negotiating. Are you getting into discussions of money too quickly?

Third, review your **SODAR** stories. Practice them out loud and tape yourself. Do what actors do, go over and over your verbal presentation. Practice does make perfect!

Fourth, are there objections coming up that you are not handling properly? If you have any doubts, review our ARTS and ICEBERG techniques in Chapter 12 and improve your responses to the situations you now know will arise.

Fifth, go back over our list of common interview questions and check all of the ones that you have been asked. Then, take the time to verbalize out loud the best answers you can develop. If you have the time, type your answers to the ones that bother you the most. Then, read them out loud and make revisions until you are totally comfortable.

Review our chapter on building your will to succeed and its implications for your personal situation. As we point out, success is inevitable for 95% of all job seekers. It's only a matter of when you make it happen.

Section Six: Reference

This last section of this System includes a range of general reference information that may only be of interest to people in special situations. The subjects discussed include how to handle liabilities, the importance of building your will to succeed, how to make professional outplacement work best for you, and reference sources for information .

How to Handle Any Personal Liabilities

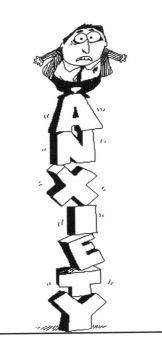

Three out of four people lose a job at least once during their career, and the higher you go, the greater the risk.

Introduction

Virtually everyone who becomes unemployed becomes re-employed. However, some do it quickly and successfully while others struggle, give up on themselves and settle for poor positions.

Today, unemployment is looked at from a far different perspective than in years past. For the most part, someone who becomes unemployed is viewed as a victim of economics beyond anyone's control.

Nevertheless, for those who lose their jobs, there can be a feeling of shock, disbelief and even fear. It can mean the loss of many symbols of security that we often take for granted. When we have a job, we have a place to go, an opportunity to achieve, tasks to fill our work day and people to work with, including close friends.

Even in those cases where people resign, their initial feelings of self-confidence can quickly give way to concern and doubt if they don't land a suitable new job quickly. Obviously, loss of income can also cause great apprehension.

Other people may not admit it and may be quick to claim they quit all their previous positions, but it is likely that many executives who will interview you will have shared the same experience at some stage in their career. In fact, it is a rare individual who can succeed in moving ahead without being fired at least once during his career.

Being fired, or asked to leave, doesn't mean failure in the eyes of everyone else, even though you may feel tremendously depressed. Don't let it give you a complex, and even more important, don't feel sorry for yourself.

Being unemployed does mean that you'll be carrying a handicap. Regardless of the circumstances, the great majority of firms prefer candidates who are presently employed.

The eight key steps you need to take

Your ability to bounce back will be a true test of your basic strength. If you do find yourself in a position of having suddenly lost your job, you might consider the following:

Register for unemployment. Don't let your pride stand in the way of accepting a weekly unemployment check. Almost everyone who loses a job ends up being unemployed for much longer than expected.

Don't vacation and don't hide. Start on your campaign immediately, exercise regularly and be as active as you can. Your advantage will be your ability to devote your entire effort to job hunting.

Get access to an office phone. It helps to have a base of operations at an office. You might be able to use the number of a friend who can have his secretary take messages for you, or list a phone number (separate from your home phone) under your own consulting service. At the very least, establish a work station in your home, and let everyone know it is to be treated as your office.

Get yourself a mentor. You will need someone who is a source of encouragement and who can be a good sounding board. It can be a relative, friend or associate whom you respect. Share your progress with that person and maintain communication throughout the campaign.

Get support from your employer. In addition to outplacement assistance, they might even provide office space, secretarial help and the use of a phone. Get total agreement on the reason for your separation. If there were negatives involved, work out an explanation which puts you in the best possible light. Look for clarification that the termination was due to factors beyond anyone's control, such as a cutback, merger or reorganization.

Get agreement that you had been a valuable contributor, and where it applies, that the final separation was arrived at jointly. Explain that you did not want to look for a job or take a lesser position while drawing a paycheck.

One last point about relationships with your most recent employer. Don't make the mistake of implying threats or communicating negatively. If you are in a position to harm your employer, they will know about it without your saying so; and they'll be taking it into account in dealing with you.

Invest in your campaign. If you lose your job, start investing in your campaign right away. Review the chapter on outplacement and see if your past employer will pay for the cost. If the answer is no, you haven't lost anything.

You should also complete a financial plan which assumes that you may be unemployed for the next six months. In the course of planning, make sure you eliminate all unnecessary entertainment and household luxuries. However, allow sufficient funds to enable you to dress well, to get any professional help you need, and to actively pursue a first-class job campaign.

Don't be overanxious. Never beg for a position and never try to explain your present situation in print. Everyone likes to hire talent that is hard to find. Don't show up in advance of your scheduled interviews, and don't always be available at the first suggested time for further interviews.

Be as active as you can. Many people who have not been active have found that the more time passed, the less capable they were—psychologically and emotionally—to go out and do what must be done to win their new jobs.

The best psychological boost you can get will come from having a schedule of full activity: breakfast meetings, business lunches, interviews, letter writing, phone calls, follow-ups and negotiations.

The way to do that is to get into action and give your job search top priority. This is no time to start fixing up the house! Develop a discipline just as if you were going to work. Here's a brief list of other common pitfalls to watch out for when you are unemployed.

Don't fail to accept introductions. Most people like to help their friends and it's foolish not to give them the opportunity.

Don't be unwilling to relocate. Sometimes it's better to go where the action is, and most people can adjust far better than they realize.

Don't feel sorry for yourself. You'll end up being the only one hurt by these emotions.

Be willing to consider a career or industry change. If your present occupation or industry is on the decline — now is a good time to make your move.

Don't allow your health to slip. Attitude and physical fitness go hand in hand.

Other job hunting problem areas

As important as your assets and skills are, you also need to be aware of anything that might be viewed as a shortcoming in the eyes of potential employers. Sometimes liabilities are overlooked. On other occasions they are mistakenly thought to be so serious that job hunters conclude that no corrective action can be taken.

To be successful, you should develop your strategy for handling any potential liability before you ever write your resume or get involved in interviews. Here is a list of the most common problem areas for people seeking new jobs. You may wish to check those that might be considered liabilities in your situation. Once you've identified them, give some careful thought relative to how you should minimize their impact in all of your communications... both written and verbal.

❑ You are unemployed
❑ You have narrow experience
❑ Your industry experience is unrelated to your goals
❑ You have stayed too long with one employer
❑ You may be too old
❑ You have changed jobs too often
❑ You may be too generalized
❑ You have been a homemaker raising a family
❑ You may be too young
❑ Your career has peaked
❑ Your achievements are not measurable
❑ Your earnings are relatively low
❑ You have been passed over
❑ You lack experience in large firms
❑ You may be too specialized
❑ Your jobs are all similar
❑ You need to relocate
❑ You may not have the right education
❑ You don't have management experience
❑ Your work history has gaps

Keep in mind that there is virtually no career problem that has not already been successfully resolved by someone else. As you review these pages, you will soon realize that any liability can be overcome if you will commit to taking actions that will resolve them.

Besides covering unemployment in this section, if you have narrow experience or need to make a career change, you can benefit from a review of our discussion in Chapter 2.

Staying too long with one employer

There was a time when people expected to work for only one or two employers in their careers. Staying with the same company for many years was not only a sign of loyalty but also a source of pride. The trend in the opposite direction has accelerated with each recession.

Today it is not uncommon for corporations to find themselves forced to lay off valued employees who have performed well. As a result, fewer and fewer achievers are overstaying their welcome. They are taking action before it's too late.

Obviously, times and values are changing and staying in one company for a long time is not the asset it once was. In fact, even when you have switched employers, if you stayed in the same job for five years or more, it will probably be considered a negative.

To make sure that you don't suffer from such perceptions, try to structure your resume so that your experience and achievements emphasize a broad range of talents and accomplishments. Prove that you have been effective with both your associates and superiors.

Normally, in situations where a person has worked for one company for a long time, the challenges have varied. If this is true, be sure to point it out. You may have had what amounted to many interesting jobs, even if you held just one title in one company.

When you take inventory of your situation, be honest with yourself. Why have you been in one company too long? Have you lost your ambition and flexibility, or was your employer able to offer you a series of interesting tasks? More often than not, you will find it is the latter.

If you've lost a sense of challenge and excitement, that's all the more reason to get moving. Further delays will only deepen the problem. You will probably be surprised at how simple it is to overcome this liability, once you decide to move on it.

Many people run the risk of staying too long in one job as a result of inertia. Very often, talented professionals will take the easy way by staying put. Years pass, and they suddenly realize that it is time to break the pattern.

Whenever you have long tenure with one employer, it serves as testimony that you have been effective for that employer. They kept you on because you delivered needed results. Sell those results.

Long tenure also helps clarify that you are a compatible individual who gets along with superiors, peers, subordinates, suppliers, customers and others. Final hiring decisions are usually based upon compatibility.

When it comes to marketing yourself, you need to show your adaptability by playing up your ability to manage and deal with change. Have you changed departments? Were you transferred on occasion? Did you serve in different divisions? Have you had a number of bosses? Do you know more than one product line? All of this information can be important in positioning yourself in a more positive fashion.

You can take the initiative by pointing out that, at various times, your responsibilities actually fit quite distinct job titles. Sometimes the very nature of the company's growth, expansions and diversification can help you project an image as a versatile performer.

Communicate how you have helped your employer increase revenues, profits, assets, market share, etc. Take partial credit for the winning moves of the team you were on. Few things are accomplished by one individual. Teamwork is what produces results. If you were there, you earned the right to claim participation in delivering beneficial results.

When a company has undergone significant changes during your time there, this should be emphasized in your oral and written communications. You can think in terms of, "We achieved this goal, acquired that company, started this business, etc." even if you were not personally responsible for those actions.

Also, remember there are lots of positive aspects to working for one company for a long time, not the least of which is that you are loyal, stable and will not skip from company to company.

A long tenure with one employer constitutes strong evidence that you have been both effective and compatible. You can share your pride in your staying power and a long record of contributions. A positive mental attitude will play an important role in dealing with this liability successfully.

When you think you may be too old

In job seeking, older age can certainly prove to be a negative. However, it is quite unfortunate that so many unhappily employed people believe they are too old to change jobs. Even though they may not consciously realize it, the truth is that many use age as a convenient excuse. Most of the time they either lack the confidence to try, don't know how to go about it, or are not willing to go through the work.

At a senior age, winning a new job is never a simple task. However, despite difficulties in adjustment, a good change can bring you a totally new feeling about life. The excitement of new work, a new location and new associates, may provide a mental stimulation that helps you feel years younger.

In the mid-1980s, the job market seemed to be placing an ever-increasing emphasis on youth. However, in the 1990s, there has been a definite shift toward the favoring of experience over youth. If you happen to be one of the people who thinks he is too senior, you might briefly reflect on this.

At the same time, appreciate that you have accumulated experience that could be of value to literally thousands of firms. Your major concern should not involve whether or not to seek a job. The key question is simply how and what to communicate to the right people in the right companies.

What does being too old really mean? In the United States half of the population is over 33. To some people, being too old is being over 40, 50, or even 60. To be sure, as you get older, job hunting will become more difficult, particularly in certain fields and industries.

However, age problems in job hunting are relative. Being too young could mean that you're 45 and shooting for a top spot in an industry where 90% of the top executives are 10 years your senior. On the other hand, being 35 could be too old in the advertising field, if you have not made your mark.

Age becomes a barrier at that point when you mentally accept it as an obstacle. You should have very little difficulty finding a way to persuasively state some accomplishments that imply "I can do the same thing, or more, for you."

In most cases, you will have to rely more on letters than resumes, since letters can be more easily slanted to cover your age, length of experience and dates.

You will find it useful to make a point of stressing your sound business judgment, your ability to work in any type of environment and your drive (which is, of course, what many believe senior people do not possess).

Sell your maturity and depth of experience. As far as your resume is concerned, avoid mentioning your age. As a general rule, emphasize only recent work (the last ten years at a maximum). You can, if appropriate, disclose your age during the interview.

As you become older, your need to make a good first impression will become even more vital. If you're out-of-shape and run-down, change your diet and consider exercising under a doctor's direction. Naturally you will need to make sure that your appearance is at its best.

How to Build a Will to Succeed That Makes the Difference

Approach success as being inevitable. Your positive attitude is what can help you do it sooner rather than later.

Develop totally positive beliefs about yourself

A positive attitude is the single most common thread among all winners. It separates people from the tens of thousands who simply give up, settle for less or remain in unattractive situations. It's easy to build a will to succeed if you're ready to work at it.

Now, it won't be news to you that if you truly believe in yourself, you will have the best possible chance of achieving the most you are capable of. So it's a good time to remind yourself of all of the good things you have done, and what you can do in the future.

Where would you get these ideas? It starts with your past, naturally. When you look at your past, start with what psychologists have called "selective perception;" namely, concentrate on the positive things and ignore the negative. One way to do this is to write down positive things you've done. All you need are short sentences.

Here are some examples: I have increased profits; I have attracted new business; I have improved systems; I have cut costs; etc. If you are a recent graduate or a returning home-maker, your "have done" list should relate to your own environment. For example: I have graduated from college; I have achieved a B average; I have managed a household budget; I have been a fund-raiser; and so forth.

Now you should go on to make another list — your next step in working on your beliefs. The idea here is to list positive things you "can do." For example: I can get along well with people; I can analyze complex facts; I can get things done quickly; I can get people to cooperate with me, etc.

Once you've prepared the above lists, you will begin to realize just what value you will have for your next employer.

Get rid of any negative beliefs

Your second step is to get rid of beliefs that might inhibit your will to succeed.

Write down any negatives and weigh them carefully. Are you thinking or saying, *"Things are bad, but this is the way they really are. There is no pie-in-the-sky for me. It's a grim world out there."*

Psychologists tell us that the beliefs we hold have a lot to do with the kind of world we experience. If, for example, you believe the economy is bad and firms are not hiring, you will go through the news and pay attention to items about layoffs or declines in sales.

On the other hand, if you believe that there are many areas of opportunity, then you will seek out new companies, new products and the like.

So, look again at your negative thoughts. Then start to realize that you can change your beliefs about the way things are. It's very simple. Write down the positive side of every negative belief. You will be left with positive beliefs, which is where you want to be.

If you have a problem in this area, search out the good news. It's always there, and it's up to you to find it and focus on it. If you go through this whole book, launch your campaign and are still battling negative thoughts, then consider getting some psychological help. You'll never achieve what you're capable of in the market until you've developed a positive attitude.

Set your expectations higher and put them to work

Here again, psychologists tell us that our expectations have a lot to do with the way things happen for us. The most dramatic examples are the athletes who when asked about their success, often reply, "We expected all along that we would win."

A look at the lives of leaders in almost any field also reveals a common theme. Whether it's a leading scientist, educator, salesperson, movie personality, or leader of industry, you'll find that each of them had very positive expectations of himself.

Inspirational leaders tell us that it is possible to work on our expectations by using internal visualization. You can practice visualizing good things happening to you. What we used to call day dreaming, experts now call "positive imaging."

Most experts suggest that you set aside a short period each day for visualizing. Picture yourself setting and achieving high goals, cutting costs, hiring other good people to work for you, bringing in new business and more.

Whatever you choose for your positive visualizations, the important thing is to work on them every day. They will give you a new-found power and self-confidence.

Project a positive attitude to everyone

If you'll follow the three steps we've discussed so far, you can develop a confident self-image and positive expectations about the future. However, now you need to project some of those internal positives to the outside world.

You can start by talking to people about your positive expectations. When you do this, it reaffirms your own commitment. You have put yourself on the line. You've let others know that you are committed to achieving your goals. Let these ideas flow into your general attitude, and begin to do as much as you can to help others.

Why? Once again, experts tell us this is a give-and-get world. When you see yourself doing things that help other people, it starts a back-and-forth movement of energy that grows.

It slowly builds momentum until it reaches the point where it becomes obvious to anyone who meets you that you project a certain confidence and a good feeling about yourself.

This, in turn, helps create the kind of environment where people make positive decisions about hiring. You'll have to work at this, but it's easy and it's fun.

Good posture, a spring in your step, a firm handshake, a confident look in your eye and comments which reveal a positive outlook can all help you project your inside positives to the outside world.

A brief review of self-esteem, stress and the mind-body link

I would like to share with you a few important observations about people who succeed far beyond their original expectations. Now in these situations there are obviously many variables that help bring out unusual success. However, two stand out.

One of them is the ability to recognize and act on opportunities. That was discussed in our chapter on finding unadvertised jobs. The other has to do with the ability to overcome setbacks and stress, and build self-esteem to levels that propel individual success.

Some people seem to possess a unique ability to constantly send themselves positive, healthy messages that add meaning to their lives. These people overcome fear of failure by simply coming to grips with themselves.

In essence, they build their self-esteem by acknowledging their mistakes, weaknesses and downfalls. Rather than denying them, they discover positives (as discussed in Chapter Two) and remind themselves of and take pride in even their smallest personal, social or business triumphs. I've observed that with successful people it isn't the size of the triumph that counts; these people recognize small victories and good things about themselves and keep them in the forefront of their minds.

When it comes to job hunting, the people who succeed through building self-esteem also seem to do so by almost creating some form of self-love, by liking what they are and the stage of life where they are, rather than wanting to be in someone else's shoes.

Time and time again, I have seen people succeed because they simply believed they could and others fail because they thought they couldn't. Once they've got their focus, certain people also seem to literally be able to "will" their success. Like competitors in any field, these people manage to psych themselves up and get into a routine that enables them to put forth amazing energy in pursuit of the right job.

This is not to say they are unrealistic. They look over the field, think things through, and then somehow arrange things in their lives to facilitate their focus on job hunting. This is a key difference between them and many good people who want a new job but never seem to get going. This is especially important, because when you're coping with unusual stress, the mind can only dwell on one thing at a time, and you need to make it something good that enables you to be in action.

These people I am speaking about, the ones who achieve both unusual and unexpected success, also constantly motivate and remotivate themselves by setting goals, and by focusing only on what they can control. For example, a common thread I've recognized is that they never waste time making excuses about competitors— people they might perceive as better looking, more poised or having better qualifications— *because that is something they can't control.*

They also turn their long-term job hunting goal into a *mini-series of short-terms goals* so they can be succeeding along the way. They psych themselves up by achieving something every day, and it keeps them feeling good about themselves. Sometimes it's just making ten phone calls or getting out ten answers to ads, and things of that sort.

Another similarity among these people is their ability to concentrate. Like top athletes who have a string of good performances, they seem to catch the flow. They clear their minds, ignoring anything that might otherwise distract them from achieving daily goals.

As previously discussed, mental imagery, or being able to visualize positive things happening, is also common to these people. It works here just as it does for athletes who are trying to set a high jump record or sink a putt at the U.S. Open. Rehearsing various positive scenarios in your mind can have a dramatic impact on your success.

The last point I would like to make relating to these people has to do with feeling good physically. Here as well, certain people simply make themselves feel better. For example, I am referring to people who may have been out of shape or in good shape, but who then vary or add to their routine by starting to run every day, or who start taking vitamins such as C, E, Beta-carotene, etc.

Now, this is not written from scientific evidence, but whatever they do, within days I've seen people believing they are feeling better, sometimes after months of feeling down, and then translating that into other actions which helped speed their ultimate success.

Make things happen by simply getting into action

Too many people make excuses for not getting into action. If it's not a recession, then it's the problems of their industry. If not that, then their skills have become obsolete by technology. If not that, there are too many people going after too few jobs.

There is no end to the power of rationalizing. Of course, these people lose their will to succeed and become immobile.

If, on the other hand, you look at the lives of achievers in any field, you will see that in addition to positive expectations, another common thread is they are very active people.

Taking action is in itself like taking an energy tonic. When people get into action on anything, they no longer have time to worry about whether they will achieve their goal.

Choose any kind of example you like. The head of a college breathing new life into an institution, a company president turning around a bankrupt operation, a football coach turning a losing team into winners, or a test pilot setting a new speed record. They are so intent on their actions, there is no room for doubt and indecision.

Don't let life go by without doing the things you really want to do. To get the right new job you need the right attitude to get going and the determination to do your best. Then you need to project the right attitude with everyone you meet. In short, it's your attitude that makes the sale. It works!

How to Select an Outplacement Firm That's Best for You

Professional outplacement: How to choose a service that is right for you

The term outplacement was first coined more than 25 years ago. While many people retain outplacement services privately, the term itself generally stems from the process whereby employers sponsor job search assistance for employees they terminate.

 Now you might ask why employers would pay to help people when they are downsizing. They begin with the difficulty of letting people go. Many employers provide this service because they want to ease the process.

Others provide it to reduce legal exposure and to show those who remain that the company treats people fairly. Still others provide outplacement to keep good public relations and, of course, to help people get reemployed with less stress and bad feelings.

Today, private and corporate outplacement is a billion dollar industry and growing rapidly each year. Unfortunately, the term itself can easily mislead people. Outplacement services involve helping people help themselves to find a new job. No one does it for you or places you! Until recently, most services simply involved having a counselor teach you about job hunting and then continue as a sounding board throughout your search. However, the biggest development in outplacement involves firms that really help market you.

There are a lot of good outplacement consultants— but the nature of their services and the resources at their disposal can differ dramatically. Here's what to look for when you consider selecting an outplacement firm.

■ **Counsel and mentoring support.** The most important thing outplacement firms do is to provide for the availability of their professional counsel. Having a knowledgeable consultant in your corner— every step of the way— can make an enormous difference. Be sure to ask if the service includes this on an unlimited basis until you get a job.

■ **Products which cover the latest job change techniques.** Ask if you can see the materials which are supplied to you as part of their service. They are normally supplied for your permanent reference, and the most reputable firms will be happy to oblige you. If they say they don't have any materials, it's a signal that they may be spending their professional time simply teaching basics.

■ **Identification of your career and industry options.** This is an important part of any first-rate outplacement service. Besides presenting their recommendations, they may provide some testing for career direction that might be helpful to some.

■ **Your action plan for generating interviews.** Any outplacement firm should draft your action plan and present it to you in a consultation. Advanced services will put all of their key recommendations in writing.

■ **Professional writing services.** Many firms, including some national organizations, are strictly counseling oriented and only guide you in preparation of your own materials. A second classification of firms will help draft a single resume for you.

However, the most advanced services offer full professional copywriting assistance. Be sure to ask if the firm completely handles the writing of all required resumes and the initial drafting of all recommended letters. Also ask to see a full set of the creative materials they have written for another client, and judge for yourself how impressive their work may be. *It takes any good professional up to 20 hours to turn out a full set of several resumes and drafts of 10 letters.*

■ **Computer research on employers and recruiters to contact.** This involves developing all of the initial information on employers and recruiters to contact as part of your telemarketing and direct mail campaign. Many outplacement firms will leave this for you to do. Others will talk about research, but when you pin them down, they really only let you use resources in their libraries.

The most advanced firms maintain the best computer databases available, and they will have their research staff run off the various reports you require.

■ **Spot opportunity reports.** This research service can be of great help if your interest is in a single metropolitan area. Here the outplacement firms have their research staffs review all of the business press on a daily basis. They search out any news event which might be a lead to unadvertised opportunity, and enter into their database.

When you become their client, they can instantly provide you with an "events report" that gives you hundreds of potential leads and brings you current on what's been happening in the local marketplace for the last six months. If you are relocating to an area where you don't have a network this can be especially valuable.

■ **Video interview training.** You may find yourself quite rusty in interviews. In just a single session, a good consultant can help you correct bad habits and project your best possible image.

■ **Campaign implementation options.** While generally available as an optional service, you can have most outplacement firms print enough stationery, envelopes and resumes to help you get into action quickly.

A more significant option can involve their implementing your direct mail campaign to recruiters and employers. This can mean doing the word processing, envelope stuffing and stamping of hundreds of pieces. If you are a senior executive, a full professional search on a national level can involve selective direct mail marketing to up to 3,500 employers and recruiters.

■ **Office space and administrative support.** If you are out of work or about to be, having access to office space, phone and word processing services can be a great advantage. If it's offered, be sure to check out the facilities before you decide to accept the service.

■ **What outplacement services cost.** The cost for group sessions can range from $300 per person for workshops, to $950 for advanced courses.

Full private "counseling only" services had cost 10% to 15% of annual compensation. However, in recent years higher volume and aggressive competition have reduced fees dramatically. Human resource professionals now purchase counseling services at levels averaging 6% to 7.5% of annual income. Then, they add whatever extras they feel are appropriate.

In dollar terms this means typical fees for a full outplacement "counseling" service will cost $2,500 to $3,000 up to the $40,000 level; $3,500 to $4,000 up to the $60,000; and $5,000 at levels for people earning or seeking up to $100,000. Even at more senior levels fees for a full "counseling only" service should never exceed $7,500.

(The above numbers are often exclusive of professional writing and individual research services, although more aggressive firms may include them. Office space, printing, secretarial support and campaign mailing services are also extra. Be wary of firms that won't show you their fee schedule, and who don't have detailed literature. As with other fields, some firms will charge what the traffic will bear.)

■ **Making your final selection.** Critics of corporate-sponsored outplacement point out that from an individual's standpoint, the trouble is that it's a service bought by someone other than the person being serviced.

This is a valid concern. Even some "Fortune 100" companies have been known to routinely spend money with firms in their old boys' network —without buying the most service they could get for their money for their departing employees. Today, most knowledgeable human resource professionals in this field will advise you to ask to select your own outplacement firm.

Also, be sure to visit each firm's facility, assess their professionalism and their resources. As mentioned earlier, make sure they give you literature describing their service, and be wary if they don't have any or say they don't use any. When you do look at their material, review it carefully. If they don't do an impressive job of marketing themselves, they'll never do any better for you!

Warranties. Do they warranty your satisfaction with every phase of their service? If you are not satisfied, will they do the work over again until you are satisfied? If the campaign, they design does not work, will they develop a new campaign, and supply you with all new resumes, letters and research?

You should expect these warranties from any reputable firm you select, and they should give you confirmation of their warranty in writing.

The value of having the right outplacement firm behind you. With the right marketing team supporting you, professional outplacement can be a service that saves you an immense amount of time. It can also affect the life of you and your family in a way that very few services can do.

Reference Information That Can Speed Your Search

Popular occupations in the 1990s

For younger and mid-level professionals there are more career alternatives than ever before. *The Dictionary of Occupational Titles* is continuously expanded and contains over 22,000 different job possibilities.

Nevertheless, we have found that the vast majority of all younger professionals who decide on a career, or who make career changes, end up choosing among a few hundred careers that are very popular today.

If you are at a stage where you are a candidate for a new career, you should go through the list on the next few pages and check any listing that might have appeal to you. Many people find that their experience falls within several categories. Obviously, many require specialized education, training or knowledge, but our purpose in providing you with this list is to simply help spark your thinking as to possibilities over either the short or long term.

❏ Accountant/CPA	❏ Computer Programmer	❏ Film Producer
❏ Actor	❏ Computer Op. Mgr.	❏ Film Producer Asst.
❏ Actuary	❏ Computer Engineer	❏ Financial Analyst
❏ Acquisition Analyst	❏ Computer Operator	❏ Financial Planner
❏ Admin. Assit.	❏ Comp. Graphics Spec.	❏ Financier
❏ Administrative Analyst	❏ Construction Engineer	❏ Fish/Wildlife Specialist
❏ Advertising Manager	❏ Consumer Rel's Mgr	❏ Fitness Consultant
❏ Aerospace Engineer	❏ Contract Administrator	❏ Flight Attendant
❏ Agricultural Inspector	❏ Copywriter	❏ Flight Engineer
❏ Agricultural Scientist	❏ Corporate Planner	❏ Floral Designer
❏ Air Traffic Controller	❏ Correctional Officer	❏ Forestry Technician
❏ Animal Trainer	❏ Cosmetologist	❏ Franchise Management
❏ Anthropologist	❏ Courier	❏ Free-lance Writer
❏ Appraiser	❏ Credit/Loan Manager	❏ Fund Raiser
❏ Architect	❏ Cruise Director	❏ Funeral Director
❏ Art Director	❏ Cryptologist	❏ General Manager
❏ Artist/Illustrator	❏ Dancer	❏ Geologist
❏ Astronomer	❏ Database Manager	❏ Geriatric Specialist
❏ Athletic/Pro. Coach	❏ Day Care Counselor	❏ Gerontologist
❏ Auditor	❏ Decorator	❏ Glamour Photographer
❏ Author	❏ Designer	❏ Golf Club Manager
❏ Banker	❏ Dentist	❏ Graphic Designer
❏ Bankruptcy Attorney	❏ Desktop Publisher	❏ Hazardous Waste Mgr.
❏ Biologist	❏ Desktop Publ'g Oper.	❏ Groundskeeper
❏ Biofeedback Specialist	❏ Detective	❏ Health Care Manager
❏ Biomedical Engineer	❏ Developer	❏ Health Therapist
❏ Biotech. Researcher	❏ Development Officer	❏ Health Svc. Admin'r.
❏ Broadcaster	❏ Diamond Merchant	❏ Hearing Officer
❏ Building Manager	❏ Dietitian	❏ HMO Administrator
❏ Building Contractor	❏ Direct Marketer	❏ Home Economist
❏ Building Inspector	❏ Distribution Manager	❏ Horticulturist
❏ Business Analyst	❏ Economist	❏ Hospital Administrator
❏ Business Planner	❏ Editor	❏ Hotel Manager
❏ Business Programmer	❏ Education Admin.	❏ Human Resource Mgr.
❏ Buyer/Purch'g Agent	❏ Electrical Engineer	❏ Importer
❏ Cash Manager	❏ Electro-opt'l Engineer	❏ Industrial Designer
❏ Ceramic Engineer	❏ Electronics Engineer	❏ Industrial Engineer
❏ Chef/Gourmet Chef	❏ Embassy Manager	❏ Insurance Adjuster
❏ Chem. Depend. Spec.	❏ Employment Agent	❏ International Acct.
❏ Chemical Engineer	❏ Engineer Technician	❏ International Courier
❏ Chemist	❏ Entrepreneur	❏ International Lawyer
❏ Child Care Manager	❏ Environmental Analyst	❏ Interpreter
❏ Chiropractor	❏ Environ'l. Attorney	❏ Investigator
❏ Cinematographer	❏ Environ'l. Engineer	❏ Investment Banker
❏ City Housing Manager	❏ Environ'l. Spec.	❏ Investment Manager
❏ City Manager	❏ Escrow Officer	❏ Jeweler
❏ Civil Engineer	❏ Estimator	❏ Journalist
❏ Clinical Rsch.Asst.	❏ Executive Recruiter	❏ Labor Relations Mgr.
❏ Collection Mgr.	❏ Executive Assistant	❏ Labor Negotiator
❏ Comptroller	❏ Facilities Manager	❏ Labor Organizer
❏ Computer Manager	❏ Family Couns'g Mgr.	❏ Lab Technician
❏ Commercial Artist	❏ Fashion Events Mgr.	❏ Land Developer
❏ Comm'y Affairs Mgr.	❏ Fashion Merchandiser	❏ Landscape Architect
❏ Compensation Analyst	❏ Fast Food Manager	❏ Law Enforcement Off.

- ❏ Lawyer
- ❏ Legal Secretary
- ❏ Library Manager
- ❏ Loan Officer
- ❏ Lobbyist
- ❏ Mgmt. Consultant
- ❏ Marine Biologist
- ❏ Marketing Analyst
- ❏ Marketing Manager
- ❏ Materials Manager
- ❏ Mathematician
- ❏ Mechanical Engineer
- ❏ Media Buyer
- ❏ Medical Investor
- ❏ Medical Secretary
- ❏ Medical Technician
- ❏ Mental Health Couns'r.
- ❏ Merchandiser
- ❏ Metallographic Tech.
- ❏ Metallurgical Engineer
- ❏ Meteorologist
- ❏ Microbiologist
- ❏ MIS Manager/Director
- ❏ Motion Picture Director
- ❏ Musician
- ❏ Network Specialist
- ❏ Network Operator
- ❏ New Product Specialist
- ❏ Nuclear Specialist
- ❏ Nuclear Engineer
- ❏ Nutritionist
- ❏ Nursing Administrator
- ❏ Occupational Therapist
- ❏ Oceanographer
- ❏ Office Manager
- ❏ Optical Technician
- ❏ Optometrist
- ❏ Outplace't. Counselor
- ❏ Paralegal
- ❏ Park Ranger
- ❏ Personnel Specialist
- ❏ Petroleum Engineer
- ❏ Pharmacist
- ❏ Photographer
- ❏ Physical Therapist
- ❏ Physician
- ❏ Physician's Assistant
- ❏ Physicist
- ❏ Pilot
- ❏ Planning Specialist

- ❏ Podiatrist
- ❏ Political Analyst
- ❏ Political Scientist
- ❏ Politician
- ❏ Preschool Management
- ❏ Preschool Teacher
- ❏ Private Banker
- ❏ Private Investigator
- ❏ Probation Officer
- ❏ Producer
- ❏ Product Manager
- ❏ Production Planner
- ❏ Production Supt.
- ❏ Professional Athlete
- ❏ Professor/Instructor
- ❏ Property Manager
- ❏ Public Administrator
- ❏ Public Relations Spec.
- ❏ Publisher
- ❏ Quality Control Inspector
- ❏ Rabbi/Minister
- ❏ Radio/TV Announcer
- ❏ Radiologic Technician
- ❏ Radiology Manager
- ❏ Railroad Engineer
- ❏ Real Estate Broker
- ❏ Recreational Director
- ❏ Redevelop't. Specialist
- ❏ Registered Nurse
- ❏ Rehab. Counselor
- ❏ Relocation Manager
- ❏ Research Specialist
- ❏ Restaurant Manager
- ❏ Retail Store Manager
- ❏ Safety Engineer
- ❏ Sales Engineer
- ❏ Sales Trainer
- ❏ Sales Promotion Mgr.
- ❏ Sales Representative
- ❏ Sales Manager
- ❏ Service Manager
- ❏ Sanitation Engineer
- ❏ Scientific Programmer
- ❏ Scientific Writer
- ❏ Securities Analyst
- ❏ Security Consultant
- ❏ Security Director
- ❏ Seminar Presenter
- ❏ Ship's Officer

- ❏ Singer
- ❏ Social Worker
- ❏ Social Director
- ❏ Social Researcher
- ❏ Social Scientist
- ❏ Sociologist
- ❏ Software Engineer
- ❏ Soil Scientist
- ❏ Special Events Manager
- ❏ Special Ed. Teacher
- ❏ Speech Pathologist
- ❏ Speech Writer
- ❏ Sports Event Manager
- ❏ Statistician
- ❏ Stress Reduction Spec.
- ❏ Stockbroker
- ❏ Surveyor
- ❏ Structural Engineer
- ❏ Systems Engineer
- ❏ Systems Programmer
- ❏ Systems Analyst
- ❏ Tax Specialist
- ❏ Teacher
- ❏ Technical Writer
- ❏ Technical Illustrator
- ❏ Telecom Analyst
- ❏ Telemarketer
- ❏ Theatrical Director
- ❏ Title Examiner
- ❏ Tour Escort
- ❏ Tour Guide Director
- ❏ Traffic Manager
- ❏ Trainer
- ❏ Translator
- ❏ Travel Agent
- ❏ Tree Surgeon
- ❏ TV Programmer
- ❏ Underwriter
- ❏ Union Representative
- ❏ Univ'y. Admin.
- ❏ University Dean
- ❏ Urban Planner
- ❏ Veterinarian
- ❏ Viticulturist
- ❏ Winemaker
- ❏ Works Director
- ❏ Workshop Presenter
- ❏ Writer

Some faster growing industries for the 90s

**Now this is the industry
I want to be in!**

Long-term success has a lot to do with being in a growth industry at the right time. In 1982 the personal computer industry was a one billion dollar industry. Today, it is estimated to be a 90 billion dollar industry. During this period the industry has had many ups and downs, but total employment has dramatically expanded.

While many firms have been through profit squeezes and layoffs, an individual who joined this industry during the last decade would now have a substantial range of employer possibilities competing for his talents.

Another major reason for seeking out growth industries involves their need to go outside their industry to meet their employment needs. For example, a decade ago the cable television industry was just beginning a phase of explosive growth. The CEOs of these firms could not find enough people with cable television knowledge or experience to enable them to meet their own growth objectives.

As a result, opportunities abounded for people from many varied backgrounds. These firms simply hired the best natural talent, regardless of their previous areas of expertise.

Growth industries (continued)

Electronic Components

- Semiconductors (integ. circuits)
- Semiconductors (DRAM chips)
- Programmable Memory Circuits
- Capacitors
- Resistor Networks
- Circuit Boards
- Transformers
- Power Supplies
- Connectors
- Ceramics
- Superconductors

Computer Peripheral & Storage Devices

- Personal Computers
- Microcomputers
- Super Computers
- Laptop Computers
- Laser Printers
- Terminals/Modems
- Graphic Systems
- Communication Equipment
- Reading Equipment
- Membrane Keyboards
- Disk and Tape Drives
- Magnetic Recording Heads
- Multimedia Systems
- Work Station Networks

Automation

- Robotics
- Optical Scanning Equipment
- POS Registers
- Voice Recognition Systems
- CAD/CAM
- Office Automated Equipment

Communication Equipment

- Digital Telephone Systems
- Televideo Phones
- PBX Equipment

- Cellular Phones
- Satellite Systems
- Cable TV Equipment
- Laser Systems
- Radar Systems
- Security Systems
- Microwave Systems
- Optical Fibers/Cable

Communication Services

- Satellite Systems
- Telecom Companies
- Cellular Phone Services
- Cable TV Systems
- Long-Distance Systems
- Advanced Voice System

Scientific / Medical & Instrumentation Equipment

- Environmental Controls
- Optical Instruments
- Disp. Medical Products
- Sensitive Radar
- Semiconductors
- Research
- Diagnostic Medical Equipment
- Medical Imaging
- Laser Systems
- Electronic Monitoring Systems
- Test Equipment
- Process Control Instrumentation
- Analytical Instrumentation
- Digital Instrumentation
- Water Purification Equipment
- Chemical Waste Equipment
- Air Pollution Systems
- Etching Equipment
- Drug Distribution Systems
- Microwaves

Chemicals / Pharmaceutical / Biomedical / Biological

- Cosmetic Specialties
- Anti-Cancer Drugs

- Soft-Tissue Implants
- Genetic Engineering
- Plasma Etching
- Vaccines
- Water Treatment Chemicals
- Polystyrene Resins
- Polycrystalline Resins
- Polymers
- Adhesives
- PVC Resins
- Elastomers
- Specialty Varnishes
- Bio-Tech Products

Publishers / Printers / Packaging

- Business Forms
- Newsletters
- Financial Newspaper
- Commercial Printing
- Educational Printing
- Credit Card Printing
- Phone Directories
- Specialty Book Clubs
- Self-Help Publishing
- Database Publishers
- Corrugated Boxes
- Paper Products
- Packaging Materials
- Tamper-Proof Packaging
- Plastic Packaging
- Catalog Printing

Retail

- Direct Marketing
- Franchise Fast Foods
- Drug Chains
- Gourmet Foods
- Discount Department Stores
- Convenience Stores
- Fine Arts/Antiques
- Health/Vitamin Shops
- Factory Outlets
- Mid-Level Restaurants
- Specialty Supermarkets
- Mail Order Catalogs
- Non-Food Retailing

Consumer Products

- ❏ Audio Equipment
- ❏ Laser Disc Equipment
- ❏ VCRs
- ❏ Large Screen TVs
- ❏ Microwave Ovens
- ❏ Auto Electronics
- ❏ Recreational Vehicles
- ❏ 4-Wheel Drive Autos
- ❏ Power and Sail Boats
- ❏ Off-Road Bikes
- ❏ Auto After-Market
- ❏ Home Furnishings
- ❏ Women's Business Apparel
- ❏ Men's Suits
- ❏ Energy Conservation Products
- ❏ Geriatric Products
- ❏ Athletic Equipment
- ❏ High Definition TV
- ❏ DAT
- ❏ FAX Machines
- ❏ Interactive Video
- ❏ Carbonated Drinks
- ❏ Baked Goods
- ❏ Low Calorie Wines
- ❏ Convenience Foods
- ❏ Prepackaged Diet Meals
- ❏ Low Alcohol Beverages
- ❏ Health Foods
- ❏ Pasta Products
- ❏ Security Products
- ❏ Automated Cameras
- ❏ Fine Watches/Jewelry
- ❏ Exercise Videos

Financial

- ❏ Bank Holding Co's
- ❏ Real Estate Investment Firms
- ❏ Financial Services Holding Cos.
- ❏ Health Insurance
- ❏ Investment Banks
- ❏ Financial Advis./ Investment Serv.
- ❏ Regional Banking
- ❏ Universal Life Insurance
- ❏ Consumer/Industrial Financing
- ❏ Money Market Funds
- ❏ Casinos/Gambling

- ❏ Leasing Services
- ❏ Credit Support Services

Consumer & Health Services

- ❏ HMOs & PPOs
- ❏ Outpatient Centers
- ❏ Emergency Care Centers
- ❏ Dental Care Clinics
- ❏ Psychiatric Hospitals
- ❏ Cosmetic Surgery
- ❏ Fitness Services
- ❏ Health Monitoring
- ❏ Hospital Holding Co's
- ❏ Speciality Clinics
- ❏ Trauma Centers
- ❏ Home Health Care
- ❏ Nursing Homes
- ❏ Skilled Nursing Fac's.
- ❏ Weight Loss Programs
- ❏ Spas and Clubs
- ❏ Hotel/Travel
- ❏ Self-Improvement
- ❏ Adult Education
- ❏ Landscaping
- ❏ Interior Decorating
- ❏ Video Rentals
- ❏ Day Care Programs
- ❏ Security Services
- ❏ Home Cleaning Svcs.
- ❏ Graduate Education

Business Services

- ❏ Commercial Software
- ❏ Computer Software
- ❏ DP Services
- ❏ Computer R&D
- ❏ Computer Consulting
- ❏ Environ'l Consulting
- ❏ Venture Capital
- ❏ Database Management
- ❏ Information Services
- ❏ Programming
- ❏ MIS
- ❏ Management Consulting
- ❏ Advertising
- ❏ Medical R&D Labs
- ❏ Outplacement
- ❏ Direct Mail Services
- ❏ Biotechnology R&D
- ❏ Database Publishing
- ❏ Electronic Mail
- ❏ Electr. Equip't. Service

- ❏ Recruiting
- ❏ Equipment Rental
- ❏ Temporary Help

Transportation

- ❏ Courier Services
- ❏ Overnight Delivery
- ❏ Specialized Trucking
- ❏ Charter Air Travel
- ❏ Commuter Airlines

Wholesale / Distribution

- ❏ Computer Equipment
- ❏ Industrial Goods
- ❏ Consumer Appliances
- ❏ Auto Equipment
- ❏ Telecom Equipment
- ❏ Office Equipment
- ❏ Petro Super Jobbers
- ❏ Importing
- ❏ Wholesale Clubs

Other

- ❏ Ship Building
- ❏ Road/Bridge Repair
- ❏ Mini-Mill Steel Prod.
- ❏ Water Conservation
- ❏ Fragrances
- ❏ Home Construction
- ❏ Home Furniture
- ❏ Specialty Autos/Tires
- ❏ Regional Real Estate
- ❏ Foreign Car Specialties
- ❏ Insulation
- ❏ Art Collecting
- ❏ Video/Recording Svcs.
- ❏ Travel Services
- ❏ Private Clubs/Spas
- ❏ Landscape Architects
- ❏ Home Restoration
- ❏ Sports Medicine
- ❏ Events Promotion
- ❏ Gardening Products
- ❏ Investment Advising
- ❏ Fabr. Home Building
- ❏ Solar Cells
- ❏ High-Tech Ceramics
- ❏ Leisure
- ❏ Personal Care
- ❏ Environmental Law
- ❏ Computer Law
- ❏ Entertainment Law
- ❏ International Law
- ❏ Waste Management

Some advice for executives considering an industry change

Eight out of every ten executives who are changing jobs are considering new options in terms of industry and company size. Despite our recent recession, new companies are springing up throughout America. Established organizations are re-examining the way they do business. Medium-sized companies are expanding. New industries now exist that are employing tens of thousands.

The more you appear to know about an industry, the easier it is to generate interviews. Virtually all employers look for "common ground" when hiring a new executive.

For example, do you have experience in or knowledge of similar product lines, distribution channels, manufacturing methods or problems of their industry? There can be other similarities. Consider the scope of operations, the role of advertising and promotion, the importance of the field sales organization, the influence of labor, and other related items.

Naturally, the harder it is to demonstrate knowledge of an industry, the less likely an executive is to make a move into it. That rule applies to all major disciplines: sales, marketing, finance, manufacturing and operations. It is less important in staff disciplines. Here are examples of industry changes that are commonplace.

❏ A marketing executive with a tobacco company joined a cosmetics firm. Why? Their methods of marketing are similar.

❏ The EVP of a circuit board company was recruited to become president of a firm that makes power packs. Why? These industries have similarities in manufacturing and sales, even though the products are so different.

❏ An executive of an aerospace company was recruited to become chairman of a small company that sells high-tech services to defense contractors. Why? The key was the new chairman's contacts and knowledge of the marketplace.

❏ The controller of a component manufacturer was brought in as president of a company that produces plastic packages. Why? The similarities have to do with cost control as the #1 challenge.

If you have no knowledge of an industry but have an interest in exploring situations, extra steps are recommended. The easiest way to acquire knowledge of a new industry, and thereby gain credibility for it, is to read trade publications. They will bring you up-to-date on many personnel changes, new products, information on specific companies, and the biggest challenges as seen by industry leaders.

Another way is to talk with executives already in the field. In some cases you can go further by getting more formal input, attending trade shows and the like. The most radical approach is to take a lower level job in an industry in order to acquire knowledge.

During the last decade we've witnessed declines for a succession of industries. However, don't overlook opportunities in troubled industries. Executives who have worked for firms under pressure often find they can be valuable to distributors or consulting firms. Those who learned tough lessons in competitive battles can function as veterans in any industry.

As you begin to consider industry options, you'll also need to decide whether you should take a narrow view. This is essential if there are a lot of growth companies in the industries you relate to.

However, if you are part of an industry which is suffering a decline, then you will want to adopt a broad view of your options. The more you understand the dynamics of a market, the more you can spot potential opportunities. Transition is obviously more difficult but still quite possible.

Historically, executives tend to overrate the barriers and to underrate their own abilities to make contributions in new areas in a relatively short time frame. It is, of course, up to you to take the initiative to learn something about new companies, new industries, and the problems and opportunities they face.

As you review potential industries of interest, remember that while glamorous high-tech and service businesses receive 90% of the publicity today, many executives will find far more opportunities in industries which are considered low-tech or non-glamorous by today's standards.

95% of the executives who make a major career change, select one of these 18 options.

1 Buying a franchise or license

This has become the standard alternative for hundreds of thousands of executives. The number of franchises available has multiplied dramatically as more than 4,000 companies in 120 industries offer franchises today.

About 1,000,000 investors now account for 30% of our GNP and 40% of all retail sales. The amount of money required to get started in different businesses varies greatly. In the majority of cases, some help with financing is available.

Assuming you have a reasonable net worth and are credit worthy, money is not likely to be a major deterrent. You can get started with some smaller franchises for as little as $25,000. This could include businesses such as recruiting, mailbox services, and some travel agencies.

In these cases, personal "hands-on" sales and new business development skills will be the most important ingredient for success. Of course, the popular fast-food franchises will often require a commitment of $500,000 or more. Recruiting, training and management skills are the key here.

For those who can go beyond this level of investment, some hotel and restaurant franchises involve many millions of dollars and require more complex financing arrangements.

A general partner in one of these ventures will tend to function more as an investment banker than as an operating manager. Success here is often based on the investor's ability to hire the right people to run the business for him.

A high-quality franchise makes good sense for many executives. However, there is always risk involved, and you may have to leverage your own capital with debt. If you are ready to deal with that, there are some clear-cut advantages to going the franchise route. Needless to say, you must be reasonably confident that you have the personal assets required to make the business grow.

2 Starting a new venture

Many executives have certain ideas and knowledge or have access to a manufacturing facility that can provide the basis for a new venture. This direction offers the appeal of being your own boss, challenging your creativity and satisfying other needs during your career.

Perhaps you have an idea about a product around which you can develop a marketing or business plan. Can you put together financing beyond your own investment? This can be available from venture firms, private investors or even some friends.

Regardless of the source, those who provide the capital will expect you to devote all of your hours to the success of the venture. With any new business, the amount of energy required in the early stages is substantial. There can be constant risk and stress. The potential returns, however, can be enormous. Examples of success abound these days in computers, financial services, genetic engineering, retailing, recruiting, outplacement and a variety of other fields.

In one instance, a 57-year-old executive purchased the assets of a defunct firm. With his knowledge and contacts, he was able to design an industrial pump for which he knew there were lucrative markets. His fledgling operation reached profitability shortly after its fifth month.

Another case revolves around a young merchandising executive. He developed a line of dietary desserts and sold them through retail outlets in his area. After a favorable response, he raised $5 million for national expansion and eventually became worth a hundred million. According to him, his key to success was total belief in his concept.

3 The partnership option

Many executives choose the partnership option. Experience dictates that
they work best when you choose
someone whose skills complement
your own, or who has investment
money to make a business grow.

For example, an unemployed
sales executive was introduced to a
small painting contractor who had an
excellent reputation for quality work.

Within one year, the injection of his sales talent into the
painting business led to their venture becoming dramatically
larger. In a few years, the business spread over an entire
metropolitan area. Together, the partners found a synergy and
a way to make more money than either one had ever done
independently.

In another situation, a corporate controller with experience in finance joined with the owner of a residential construction company. They formed a partnership in which the
controller used his skills in negotiating and financing to begin
developing small office parks. That was the beginning of what
ultimately became a highly successful real estate development company with diverse commercial holdings.

Another person, a manufacturing VP who had spent his
lifetime in the production of high-precision metal compo-
nents joined with a top salesman for a defense contractor. The
combination of the salesman's contacts and the executive's
abilities enabled them to start a small company, almost risk-
free. Either person on his own would probably not have been
successful.

4 Investing, buying and selling

Obviously, this alternative requires an appropriate financial position and the knowledge of a particular area, or, at the very least, a willingness to learn.

Real estate investing has become an increasingly sophisticated field. The packages may involve vacant land, commercial buildings, single- or multiple-family residences, abandoned factories, government repossessions, etc. Active investors have earned millions, but there are no guarantees, and the risk can be high.

One executive who had built a successful career in merchandising bought and sold small retail stores, each of which was doing poorly. His formula was to improve their operations, develop a special promotion program for each and then sell them off for a major profit. He was able to implement "turnaround" plans within 12 weeks and sell the businesses within one year.

Another individual had an extensive collection of fine porcelain. He used his knowledge to aggressively buy and sell various collections at a substantial gain. Most important, he thoroughly enjoyed combining his hobby with his desire to maintain a substantial income. Sometimes, interest in hobbies can lead an investor to a broader business.

One woman from the construction industry learned to capitalize on a small investment in industrial real estate. She started on a limited scale, concentrated on one geographic area and rapidly became expert in it. She never purchased anything for the long term. Her focus was on turnarounds of 12 months or less. She went on to earn more in three years than she had in all of her prior years of working.

5 Purchasing a company and arranging a buyout

This can be attractive if you feel you can truly improve the company in question. In one case, a manufacturing VP lost his job. In searching for a new position, he met the president of a manufacturer of lawn furniture.

The owner was in his 60s and wanted to find a buyer who could continue to build it. They were able to structure an agreement whereby a buy-out could take place over five years, using cash flow coupled with a fairly modest equity investment at the outset.

A young executive in the biomedical field entered into discussions with the CEO of a medium-sized firm for a position as VP marketing. However, the CEO suggested that the executive study a money-losing subsidiary to determine its potential. If he chose to, he could then buy in at a favorable price, function as its president, and purchase up to 30% of the stock in future years. This provided an opportunity for him to build equity in a firm where his own performance would determine its value.

In both of these examples, it was the ability of the executive to improve the value of the company that made the equity purchase attractive. Also, there was a relatively small down payment, which made the purchase feasible.

6 Writing

Writing with commercial opportunity in mind represents another option. Many people have aspired to write a book but never had time. Hits that have created new career directions for their authors include *Mega-trends, In Search of Excellence* and *One Minute Manager*. Hundreds of lesser known examples are published every year. A more important option for writers involves preparing articles that have a potential for being accepted by some of the country's 11,000 plus trade and business magazines.

7 Buying a smaller firm outright

Purchasing smaller companies on an outright basis can offer unique advantages to those with an entrepreneurial instinct.

For example, there are opportunities that require involvement only to the extent you desire. These might include car washes, laundromats, theaters, apartments, parking lots, etc. You can put a personal stamp on such enterprises or stay in a passive role.

Specialty stores can also be candidates for purchase. Popular choices include hardware outlets, garden shops, nurseries, sporting goods stores, marinas, and product lines such as computers, men's clothing, or even gourmet foods and wines. The possibilities could include small restaurants and inns, printing and travel services, manufacturing plants, and numerous family businesses.

If you decide on this direction, consider getting the help of a business broker. In many instances, the seller's accounting records may prove unreliable. A reputable broker can play a critical role in helping you consider a cross-section of reliable possibilities. You can stimulate your own creativity by developing a list of targets that may prove interesting.

Leveraged buy-outs of larger, public corporations have recently been in vogue. The key parties are often executives in the industry. These debt-laden transactions are definitely for the sturdy few with the contacts and the sophistication required.

One airline executive who always wanted to get away from traveling found happiness as the owner of a health foods shop. Another service industry executive earns as much as ever operating running-shoe stalls in popular flea markets, and he also plays golf several days a week.

8 Independent consulting (generalists and specialists)

The field has been expanding at a rapid rate during the past decade. Part of the reason for this is that the knowledge business as a whole has been booming. If you decide to become a practicing consultant, your perceived professionalism will be very important.

As you probably realize, thousands of executives begin thriving consulting practices each year. However, it rarely happens automatically. The first thing to recognize is that you will need some form of specialty if you are to get off to a fast start.

For those attracted to consulting, it is wise to remember that whatever knowledge you have to offer must somehow be sold. Success in this field rests squarely on your ability to attract and maintain clients. Once you are established, many clients will come through referrals. However, the biggest reason for failure in consulting is that people don't foresee the personal selling effort required.

If selling is not your suit, but you are convinced you have a lot to offer, you will have to attract one or more partners or employees who will devote their time to selling your services. Some of the most popular consulting specialties include finance, marketing, new product development, data processing and systems, executive search and outplacement, cost reduction and public relations.

There is also good activity in labor relations, electrical engineering, design and other technical disciplines. If you want a consulting business, but do not have any potential clients who will quickly retain you, then cash flow may be a problem. Allow time for getting started. Identify the organizations where what you know will be of greatest value. Later on, as your reputation grows, you can broaden your base.

9 Joining a consulting firm

There are thousands of consulting firms who can benefit from the timely addition of new talent. It is an easier way to get started than striking out on your own, and you can always benefit from the experience before becoming an entrepreneur.

General management consulting, EDP consulting, executive search and outplacement also attract many generalists each year. They can be excellent if you have an ability to attract new business. Heavy phone contact and extensive travel are drawbacks. However, the pay can be excellent.

Regardless of the type of consulting you choose, remember that special knowledge which makes a consultant valuable today may be obsolete several years later. So you need to allow time to keep current with developments in your field. If you enjoy variety and intellectual challenge, then management consulting can be your right move.

An EDP executive decided to become a partner in a 15-person consulting firm. He enjoyed immediate income, based on his ability to perform work for clients. This also allowed him to refine his skills, work closely with experienced peers, and build relationships with clients without a specific responsibility for bringing in new accounts.

10 Managing a nonprofit

Surprising to some, there are more than 20,000 trade organizations, and many are exceptionally well funded. Most trade associations are run like businesses and have similar needs. However, a few characteristics make them unique.

First, they are usually membership organizations. The top administrator— the executive director— serves the membership. Often there are widely differing views among members, so diplomacy is important. Second, the director reports to a board which is elected by the members. These boards exercise a higher degree of authority over the executive director than in a business corporation.

The board members will often represent different interests and find it difficult to agree on policies and major issues. To be successful, the executive director must bring a unified policy into focus. Persuasion and tact are essential.

Lobbying at the state and national levels is an important mission for many trade groups. That means there can be frequent entertaining. Anyone interested in this type of work should also be comfortable dealing with fund-raising and all levels of government officials and lawmakers.

Frequently, the trade association will be a primary source of news for the media. If the industry encounters controversy, you can be sure the members will expect a lot from the person at the top.

There are other nonprofits that do not fit into the above categories; for example, sports organizations, student exchange services, labor unions and others. To investigate the field, talk with officials in the state chamber of commerce or your own industry association.

11 Working in education

An increasing number of opportunities are available in the troubled but challenging field of education. There are obvious choices such as those in teaching, administration or in a combination.

On the administrative side, many executives have made major contributions in helping to keep educational institutions solvent. In many respects, education is like any other service business. People must be recruited and trained and facilities must be operated efficiently. Information systems and data processing are needed; funds must be raised and public relations must be maintained, etc.

Those with corporate experience will find they are of particular value in the graduate schools of business. In fact, a number of universities have former executives and corporate officers as professors, administrators, heads of development and fund-raising, and deans of their business schools. Here, an advanced degree is usually a prerequisite. Those who favor classroom teaching or lecturing may still find that they eventually gravitate to management.

One executive joined the faculty of a large state university with a change in lifestyle as his number-one priority. Before long, he was nominated to serve as department head. He became more active in faculty politics because the faculty was in need of leadership. Five years later, he found himself a frontrunner to be president of this 25,000-student university.

In some cases, a college administrator will have far more pressure than his corporate counterparts. Low budgets, faculty unrest, political battles and outmoded systems are all factors that have to be dealt with in educational institutions. If you decide to investigate this career area, start by talking to faculty members and administrators at your alma mater. This will help you quickly get into the swing of things.

12 Seeking a directorship

Many executives who can bring prestige and experience to smaller corporations become sought after for directorships. However, it usually takes some planning to get started. When you have served on one board, you will likely be invited to join others. That is particularly true if you have specific experience that will be apparent to nominating committees.

In fact, directorships on just three or four corporations, along with committee work, can often provide adequate income and lots of challenge. Among the largest firms, directors' fees recently averaged nearly $70,000 for 148 hours of work.

Some stock exchanges can direct you to clearinghouse services for executives interested in directorships. It is also possible to conduct a campaign aimed at existing directors, investment bankers, lawyers and CEOs, discreetly inquiring whether your services might be valuable to one or more of the companies with which they are associated.

Obviously, this avenue is most feasible for executives with strong reputations. However, even if this is not the case, it is possible to develop opportunities. Think carefully of what you have to offer that would set you apart.

If you are known as an executive who can increase productivity or cut costs, or if you have proven talents in securing financing, making acquisitions or entering new markets, then it will be easy for many board members and CEOs to envision your contributions. These openings are usually coordinated by the corporate secretary who may be a good person to get in touch with initially. Turnover tends to be at its peak in late winter and early spring, and a lengthy, superior biography is a must.

In cases like this, it is wise to decide on some limits as to how many companies you can help in this capacity. Since directorships now carry more exposure to liability, corporations no longer expect directors to serve for just a nominal sum or without proper insurance.

13 Working as a producer

Producers bring in business, for example, recruiters, stockbrokers, real estate brokers, outplacement specialists, etc. If you have contacts and need a shift, this kind of role can be attractive.

A small company president acquired special knowledge of telecommunications and within years became a nationally recognized expert.

In another situation, a former VP of advertising focused on her unique copywriting skills. She became an eminent direct mail copywriter, one of the most prolific in this high paying field. This "producer" role gave her far more satisfaction than the manager role she held for so many years.

An international financial executive concentrated on his unique expertise in the tax field. He was able to use his global tax background to become the top money earner in a small but exclusive advisory firm.

A top-ranked officer of a pharmaceutical firm parlayed his 23 years in that business into a Wall Street partnership. As a leading analyst, he became a widely respected authority.

The executive vice president of a well-known conglomerate was faced with early retirement. He combined his love of sales promotion with the use of his contacts. At age 59, he became a top sales producer for an advertising specialty distributor.

There are opportunities for producers in every discipline. The key is to focus on something you can do well.

14 Engaging in charitable work

Another area to consider is to engage in charitable work. Here the key can be to affiliate with a cause that has personal meaning. This will add an important dimension of satisfaction. Certain larger organizations are professionally staffed and will occasionally search out executives. In these cases, a reasonable income may go with the job.

However, most charities are run by small staffs with limited resources, and their purposes vary greatly. Some concentrate on raising money to combat specific medical problems, while others will have assistance programs dedicated to Third World countries.

There are organizations devoted to helping religious groups, underprivileged children and hundreds of other worthwhile concerns. Nevertheless, most face an array of similar problems.

Executives from marketing, sales and public relations will fit in most easily. Larger charities can also use those with backgrounds in general management, finance, law and administration.

15 Lecturing

The lecture circuit is open to individuals in the public eye. There are agents who, for a percentage, arrange engagements that can run up to, and even more than, $15,000 per lecture. Top rates are reserved for those with celebrity status. However, thousands of people make an interesting career out of the lecture circuit. To get started, you will have to decide on timely or interesting subjects that are appropriate for you.

16 Learning an entirely new field

If you are having trouble changing industries, or you wish to make a major shift, you may have to consider taking a lower-level position in a new field and rebuilding momentum from there.

A steel executive who lost his job in a cutback decided to start a new career in data processing. He started as a programmer while going to school at night to learn systems design. Because of his maturity and work habits, he quickly rose to project leader and then to assistant manager in the DP department. He remained for more than one year before joining a larger firm as director of the function.

In another case, a president in the chemical field lost his job. His contract prevented him from working in the industry. He studied new areas and was interested in modular housing. However, he recognized he had a "credibility gap" because he knew nothing about how these products were made.

This executive decided to learn "on the job." He started in production and quickly rose to foreman. Soon thereafter, he had a complete understanding of this new industry and saw how he could contribute. With his first-hand knowledge, he was able to pursue an executive position in this business. In less than three years, he became president of one of the fastest-growing firms.

17 Returning to an earlier activity

Most executives began their careers in a line discipline, often in a producer function. More often than not, it was their performance in these areas that propelled them upward into management.

In recent years, many successful men and women have found great satisfaction going back to what they used to do. This may involve returning to a career in accounting, sales, international business, product marketing or something else. There are hundreds of examples where this makes sense.

18 Pursuing an earlier dream

The fishing enthusiast becomes a professional sea captain; the executive who enjoys small-game hunting buys into a forest hunting preserve; the avid private pilot becomes involved in managing the local airport. Second careers abound in theater, music and the arts.

A most dramatic example of pursuing a childhood dream involves one of the world's most successful "self-made" businessmen. Within ten years of retirement, this man was able to become one of the most important art collectors in the world and one of the most knowledgeable experts in a number of collector sub-specialties.

If you are serious about any of these options, ask yourself these questions

❑ How hard do you want to work? Some individuals thrive on long hours throughout their career, while others reach a point where they want to broaden their interests.

❑ How much stress can you handle? Some executives are not affected by stress. Others reach a point where they should avoid stressful situations at all costs. Many people seek out new careers in order to escape common problems, such as politics. All too often, the concerns in one environment are replaced by similar ones in the next.

❑ How much risk do you want to take? Many executives are comfortable choosing new careers where they take some financial risk. The question you need to consider is "how much?"

❑ How important is lifestyle? Along with money, this consideration is increasingly important to most successful people. More people than ever are putting location and lifestyle ahead of career.

❑ What's your attitude about starting over? Starting over can be one of the most rewarding experiences in life, but you need to be looking forward to it with enthusiasm and confidence.

❑ Do you have concerns about loneliness? With many career options you are likely to encounter loneliness. Your own judgment and resourcefulness will become paramount.

Sources for additional information

This reference section reviews some of the more popular and useful sources of information on organizations and where to find them. The information can be helpful for developing your initial "priority list" of employers to contact and for subsequently launching your direct-mail and telemarketing efforts.

Try to take advantage of the expanding world of computer databases to create your priority list. They can save you a great deal of time and enable you to quickly launch your direct-mail and telemarketing efforts.

In some cases you can call and purchase a floppy disc or CD ROM from trade associations on a particular industry or from chambers of commerce or business periodicals that publish articles in which they rank employers by various criteria.

Typically, you can select organizations by industry, location and size and then print out information such as the company name and address, telephone number, names of CEOs and their officers by their area of specialty. A few of the more popular sources that you can look into are listed below.

❑ *Lotus One Source* at 617-577-8500.
   Through this service you can get CD-ROM discs which will contain basic data such as corporate names, phone numbers, names of officers, size of companies, etc. They also have a substantial amount of financial information, and offer summaries of recent news events that have appeared in the business press.

❑ *Dun and Bradstreet* at 201-605-6000.
   They offer the Dun & Bradstreet Million Dollar Directory through Duns Marketing Services in Parsippany, New Jersey. The information is similar to Lotus'.

❑ *Contacts Influential* at 303-292-5808.
   This is another firm which offers databases in select metropolitan areas throughout the U.S.

❑ *Career Search* at 617-449-0312.
   Operating out of Needham, Massachusetts, this firm also makes available an extensive national database that competes with Dun's and Lotus'.

Here are some database and on lineservices that can be helpful.

❑ *America On Line* at 800-827-6364.

The news and finance section offers business news and can be helpful for researching spot opportunities. They also provide stock quotes and other financial information.

❑ *BRS* at 800-955-0906.
They have a business section which offers 18 major databases.

❑ *CompuServe* at 800-848-8199.
This is a popular service that offers a very extensive range of business information.

❑ *Dialog* at 800-334-2564.
This is also among the most popular services available. They have over 450 databases including TRW Business Credit Profiles, Moody's Corporate Profiles, Disclosure On Line and various Dun & Bradstreet information. Dialog also sells CD-ROM versions of about 40 databases.

❑ *Dow Jones News Retrieval* at 609-452-1511.
This service enables you to retrieve information on a specific companies with whom you might be interviewing. The service covers everything that appears in the *Wall Street Journal, Barron's, The Washington Post* and the *Dow Jones News Service*.

❑ *The Economic Bulletin Board* at 202-377-1986.
The U.S. Chamber of Commerce offers this service. The EBB lists export opportunities and various statistics relating to employment, census and industry data.

❑ *Nexis* at 800-227-4908.
This offers information from more than 1,000 sources including Standards & Poors, Disclosure Online and Predicasts.

❑ *Newsnet* at 800-952-0122.
This covers news that appears in more than 600 newsletters and 20 news services and is basically an electronic clipping service.

❑ *Princeton/Masters*
See the end of this book for information on databases on employers and recruiters

The sources below can generally be found in major libraries.

For general information

You can use any of the directories below for basic information on companies.

❑ *The Million Dollar Directory* (Dun's Marketing Services, Parsippany, NJ)

❑ *Standard & Poor's Register of Corporations*, Directors and Executives (Standard & Poor's Corporation, New York, NY)

❏ *Encyclopedia of Bus. Information Sources* (Gale Research, Inc., Detroit, MI)

❏ *Guide to American Directories* (B. Klein Publications, Coral Springs, FL)

❏ *Ward's Business Directory* (Gale Research, Inc., Detroit, MI)

Information on recruiters

❏ *See the end of this book for information on obtaining names/addresses specialties of recruiters.*

Information on management

❏ *Reference Book of Corporate Managements* (Dun's Marketing Services, Parsippany, NJ)

❏ *Who's Who* Series (Marquis Who's Who, Inc., Wilmette, IL)

Information on industries

❏ *The Directory of Directories* (Gale Research, Inc., Detroit, MI).

If you want information about virtually any industry, this book will list the directories that either have the information you need or will guide you to it. It has two indices. One lists the names of companies alphabetically, the other classifies by subject.

❏ *SRDS Business Pub. Rates and Data.* (Standard Rates and Data, Wilmette, IL)

This monthly publication is used primarily by advertising agencies to determine the cost of advertising in a particular media. It can be useful to job seekers because it lists virtually every significant trade and professional publication in the country.

❏ *F&S Index of Corporations & Industries* (Predicasts, Inc., OH)

If you are interested in a specific industry, this lists recent articles on that industry that have appeared in business and trade journals. The second section gives you the same information according to company names.

Information by product

If you have narrowed your interest to companies that manufacture for a particular market niche, there are three sources you will find helpful. They are:

❏ *Thomas Register of American Manufacturers* (Thomas Publ. Corp., NY, NY)

❏ *Brands and Their Companies/Companies and Their Brands* (Gale Research Inc., Detroit, MI)

❏ Thomas Regional Industrial Purchasing Guides

❏ Thomas Specialized Industrial Purchasing Guides

Thomas Register is the most comprehensive source for finding all companies that make a given product.

Geographic areas

There are many publications that give detailed information about a specific metropolitan area, such as the *Becker Guide for Chicago*. Virtually every major city has such a publication. The Directory of Directories lists publications for specific geographic areas. Chambers of Commerce can also be   excellent sources of information.

Large corporations

❑ *The Fortune 1000 Directory* and similar lists published by *Inc.*, *Forbes* and *Business Week*

❑ *The Directory of Corporate Affiliations: Who Owns Whom* (National Register Publishing, Wilmette, IL)

❑ *America's Corporate Families* (Dun's Marketing Services, Parsippany, NJ)

❑ *Standard & Poor's Ultimate Parent Index*

❑ *Million Dollar Directory Top 50,000 Companies* (Duns Marketing Services, Parsippany, NJ)

❑ *Reference Book of Corporate Managements* (Duns Marketing Services, Parsippany, NJ)

If you are interested in the largest corporations within specific industries, you should also refer to the survey issues put out by *Forbes, Fortune* and *Business Week.*

Small companies

Trade publications usually contain some information on specific companies. Magazines, such as *Inc.,* provide information on small, growing companies and list larger numbers in their directory issues.

Public companies

You will find useful information in:

❑ *The Value Line Investment Survey* (A. Bernhard & Co., New York, NY)

❑ *Stock Reports* (Standard & Poor's Corp., New York, NY)

❑ *Moody's Complete Corporate Index* (Moody's Investors Service, New York, NY)

❑ *Standard Corporation Records* (Standard & Poor's, New York, NY)

❑ Annual reports to shareholders of individual companies

❑ 10K Reports on individual companies

In addition, many brokerage firms will publish reports put together by their analysts on individual industries. Contact the local office of a brokerage firm to learn how you can gain access to those reports.

Foreign companies

The most helpful sources include:

❑ *Bottin International Business Register*

❑ *The International Who's Who* (Europa Publishing, Ltd., London, England)

❑ *Directory of American Firms Operating in Foreign Countries* (Uniworld Business Publications, New York, NY)

❑ *Directory of Foreign Firms Operating in the United States* (World Trade Academy Press, Inc.)

❑ *The Exporters Directory/U.S. Buying Guide*

❑ *International Directory of Corporate Affiliations* (National Register Publishing Company, Inc., Wilmette, IL)

For specific information for a particular country, several directories may be of assistance. They include:

❏ *Dun's Latin America's Top 25,000*

❏ *Europe's 10,000 Largest Companies*

❏ *Taiwan Business Directory*

❏ *Standard Trade Index of Japan*

❏ *Key British Enterprises*

Venture capitalists

If you want to start your own business or buy a company, there are three sources that you will find helpful. Occasionally, the firms listed in these directories will need to locate management talent to run a business in which they already have an interest or which they are about to start.

❏ *The Corporate Finance Source Book*

❏ *Guide to Venture Capital Sources* (Venture Economics, Inc., Needham, MA)

❏ *National Venture Capital Association Directory*

Associations

Your background or interests may point you toward working for an association or an organization rather than a corporation. The following publications may be helpful. They are:

❏ *Encyclopedia of Associations* (Gale Research, Inc., Detroit, MI)

❏ *Business Organizations and Agencies Directory* (Gale Research, Inc., Detroit, MI)

❏ *National Directory of Addresses and Telephone Numbers*

❏ *National Trade and Professional Associations*

The Encyclopedia of Associations, published by Gale Research, includes 17 categories of organizations and associations.

Business Organizations and Agencies Directory, also published by Gale Research, contains information on trade organizations, associations, labor unions, federations, chambers of commerce, better business bureaus, federal government agencies, state agencies and news sources.

You will also find information on conference and convention bureaus, franchise companies, publishers, educational institutions, business libraries, research centers, bureaus and institutes.

❏ *The National Directory of Addresses and Telephone Numbers* contains addresses and telephone numbers of 75,000 U.S. corporations plus various government offices, hotels, colleges, banks, associations, unions, hospitals, radio and TV stations, accounting and law firms, advertising agencies, magazines, and papers.

❏ *The National Trade & Professional Associations Directory* includes associations and labor unions in the U.S. It is indexed by subject and geographic location.

❏ The survey issues mentioned earlier, published by *Fortune, Forbes* and *Business Week*, are a source of information on industry trends. Recent issues of trade publications in any field, if quickly scanned, will also give you an idea of an industry's trends and significant issues.

Index